W9-AFM-419

COUNTRY MEN

National Portrait Gallery

IZAAK WALTON
(J. Huysmans)

JOHN MOORE

COUNTRY MEN

Illustrated with eight half-tone plates and engravings after Bewick, Thurston and Nesbit

Essay Index Reprint Series

BOOKS FOR LIBRARIES PRESS
FREEPORT, NEW YORK

First Published 1935
Reprinted 1969

LIBRARY OF CONGRESS CATALOG CARD NUMBER:
69-17585

PRINTED IN THE UNITED STATES OF AMERICA

TO

FRANCIS BRETT YOUNG

NOTE

THREE of these chapters have appeared in the form of essays in the *English Review* and one other has been given, in a different version, as a talk upon the wireless. I am grateful to the editor of the *English Review* and to the B.B.C. for thus permitting them a preliminary canter before their appearance in my book. The etching of John Mytton is reproduced from Miss Edith Sitwell's book *The English Eccentrics* by permission of the publishers, Faber and Faber Ltd.

J. M.

1935.

CONTENTS

LIST OF ILLUSTRATIONS

The head- and tail-piece decorations are reproduced from the original wood-engravings by Thomas Bewick in his 'History of British Birds' (1797–1804) and from engraved illustrations by John Thurston and Charlton Nesbit to Bloomfield's 'The Farmer's Boy' (1800) and 'May Day with the Muses' (1822)

Chapter I — *Green Fields*

''A BABBLED of green fields,' said Mistress Quickly. Sir John Falstaff lay a-dying and, true enough, he shouted for sack as befitted him, and called upon God, and cried out that women were devils incarnate, but chiefly he babbled of green fields. The essential fitness of his ending seems to have impressed even Nym and Bardolph and the fantastic spidery villain that was called Ancient Pistol, for they were hushed into silence by Mistress Quickly's words. ''A parted even just between twelve and one, e'en at the turning o' the tide: for after I saw him fumble with the sheets, and play with flowers, and smile upon his fingers' ends, I knew there was but one way: for his nose was as sharp as a pen, and 'a babbled of green fields.'

After that, Nym and Bardolph and Pistol go off to France to fight for King Henry. The King blusters and waves his sword and gloriously bids them 'cry "God for Harry! England! and Saint George!"'; he threatens breached Harfleur with rape and pillage ('And the flesh'd soldier . . . mowing like grass Your fair-fresh virgins and your flowering infants'); he gushes great spouts of magnificent rhetoric upon Saint Crispin's Eve—yet somehow in the midst of all this splendid bombast there shines a memory of Sir John's death, and the green English fields.

It has always been thus. In the tumult of England's crises there have always been men who have babbled of her green fields, and whose small insistent babbling has made itself heard above the shouts of victorious mobs and the marching and countermarching of soldiers in her wars. Theirs has been a sort of whispered chronicle of little things, a tale told in undertones. It began, I think, on that April morning of showers and sunshine when Chaucer's pilgrims set out along the road to Canterbury and the small birds made melody for them. It went on through all the exciting times when Englishmen were sailing their ships to the ends of the earth, when Drake and Frobisher were beating the Spaniard and Sir Walter Ralegh was looking for El Dorado; for even in that age when poets were decorating their verses with dear-bought words from the Indies and the Americas, Michael Drayton sang the little Warwickshire rivers—'ev'ry pearl-pav'd ford and ev'ry blue-ey'd deep'—and young Gervase Markham, who wrote the stirring tale of Grenville and the *Revenge,* had time to spare also for a book of *Country Contentments,* about English fields and English weather and the trivial, pleasant things men did with horses and hawks and hounds. Shakespeare too, whose great mind ranged about the world and brought back a Cleopatra from Egypt, an Ariel and a Caliban from the Bermoothes—he never forgot the daisies pied and violets blue, nor the primroses that die unmarried in the cold English spring, nor the March winds that set the woods astir

> When daffodils begin to peer,
> With heigh! the doxy over the dale,

and though he might lay his scene in Athens or Illyria, in Venice or Navarre, the English woodlands always crept willy-nilly into it, and the humble homely flowers, and the meadows silver with lady's-smock through which the slow Avon ran from Stratford down to Fladbury and Evesham.

And so the quiet chronicle goes on. While England is at Civil War there is the gentle voice of Izaak Walton, supremely unconcerned, telling of dace and dairymaids; and Richard Franck, trooping with Cromwell, forgets psalm-singing for a while and catches salmon. And Robert Herrick, in the twilight that contains an afterglow of the splendid Elizabethan sunset, watches his Devon maids bringing in whitethorn on May Day.

After that, the babbling almost ceases; but soon there is a little parson at Selborne writing more sweetly about birds than any one had ever done before, and through a strange troubled countryside lit by the rick-fires of the Agricultural Revolution William Cobbett rides boisterously, pausing now and then to admire a good crop of swedes. And then there is George Borrow, going gustily about Wales as if he were carried along by the great winds that blow off Glyder Fawr; and then Richard Jefferies, finding new wonders in a dusty hedgerow, and W. H. Hudson, watching the birds and writing about them in such prose as a man might use who had watched the angels.

But the factories were growing up where the grass had grown, and industry was changing the face of England; in the hurry to make money and guns the green fields were almost forgotten, save by Mr. Belloc, striding over his Sussex Downs, and by a little group of young poets who, in the hush before the great storm broke over Europe, were rediscovering England almost too late. Within a year or two they were buckling on their uniform to go to the war; but they still babbled of green fields for a little longer, until one by one they died in the mud. . . .

Now that the storm is over, there seem to be fresh storms brewing yet; but the catkins still dance on the hazel-stems in March, and the moths still come to the honeysuckle in June, and the ragged robin blows in the autumn hedge. Horse-hoofs still beat out their old hexameters across the wide grasslands in November; and here and there, in the long summer evenings, men in white flannels play their preposterous lovely game on village greens. A few countrymen still care for these things, and weave tales and write verses about them; but for the most part the tales are a wistful looking-back and the poems are a requiem. Perhaps the brief episode that was English country life is nearly over, and perhaps the men who babbled of green fields will soon be forgotten. That is why I write this little book, before it is too late; lest the future belong to the machines, and the new poets who sing them.

Chapter 2 *Matins*

It is very fitting, I think, that this whispered chronicle of little things, this babbling of green fields and brooks and hedgerows, should have begun with the sound of bird-song at morning. For so it surely did, at Southwark on an April day about the year 1386,

> Whan Zephirus eek with his swete breeth
> Inspired hath in every holt and heeth
> The tendre croppes, and the yonge sonne
> Hath in the Ram his halfe cours y-ronne,
> And smale fowles maken melodye,
> That slepen al the night with open ye.

The world must have seemed very young then; and the pilgrims rode to Canterbury through a fledgeling England in which we may fancy (since grass is only as green as we think it is) that the fields looked fresher, the hawthorn-buds crisper, the spring flowers brighter than they do to-day. The pilgrims possessed that innocence and surprise which is the part of poets; they had only to look down at the roadside and they were astronomers of the new stars that shone there: stitchwort and celandine, with the hedge-parsley for a Milky Way. And the 'smale fowles,' the blackbirds and the thrushes and the linnets that sang from every bush, surely they sang as if they had made their songs for the first time upon that April day?

All the way through Chaucer's book, while the pilgrims tell their tales in turn, one has the feeling that this morning song of birds is very close at hand; it mixes with the elvish laughter that seems to have bubbled up in England then like a fresh clear spring among the hills. And one has the same sense of bird-song, and of the new wonder of it, in some of the other literature of the time: particularly, I think, in a curious and mysterious and altogether fascinating work called *The Treatyse of Fysshynge with an Angle*, which was written about a hundred years later than the *Canterbury Tales*. Perhaps it is because fishing is largely an early-morning business that we hear the birds so clearly in the *Treatyse*; here, at any rate, is a whole choir of blackbirds in the dawn:

'And yet atte the leest [the angler] hath his holsom walke and mery at his ease, a swete ayre of the swete fauoure of the meede floures: that makyth hym hungry. He hereth the melodyous armony of fowles. He seeth the younge swannes, heerons, duckes, cotes, and many other foules wyth theyr brodes; whych me seemyth better than alle the noyse of houndys; the blastes of hornys and the scrye of fowlis that hunters; fawkeners and foulers can make. And yf the angler take fysshe; surely thenne is there noo man merier than he is in his sprytes.'

Is there not in that the whole of an English morning, at the time when England was very young? And it goes merrily on:

'Also who soo woll use the game of anglynge; he must ryse erly. Whyche thyng is prouffytable to man in this wyse, That is to wyte; moost to the heele of his Soule. For it shall cause hym to be holy, and to the heele of his body, For it shall cause hym to be hole. Also the encrease of his goodys. For it shall make hym ryche. As the olde englysshe prouerbe sayth in this wyse, who soo woll ryse erly shall be holy helthy and zely. Thus have I prouyd in myn entent that the dysporte and game of anglynge is the very meane and cause that enducith a man into a mery spryte.'

There is the elvish laughter bubbling up again, a little chuckle heard amid the song of the birds; for the book has plenty of laughter in it, although it is a *Treatyse* and although it is said to have been written by no less grave a person than Dame Juliana Berners (or Barnes), Lady Prioress of

Sopwell Nunnery in Hertfordshire. This may or may not be true; there is no evidence, save tradition, in support of it. The *Treatyse* forms part of a compilation called *The Boke of St. Albans*, and it seems possible that the reverend lady may have played the part of general editor of the whole; it is, to say the least of it, unlikely that she herself wrote the minute instructions on hawking, hunting, and angling which are contained in it—instructions so detailed and intimate that they even include this hint upon the right way with maggots: 'Whan thei ben bredde grete wyth theyr naturell fedynge: ye shall fede theym farthermore wyth shepes talow & wyth a cake made of floure & hony, thenne woll they be more grete. And when ye have clensyd theym with sonde in a bagge of blanket kept hote under your gowne or other warm thyng two hours or thre, then ben they beste & redy to angle wyth.' Can this be our lady prioress, with maggots a-warming under her gown? One is inclined to doubt it. Moreover, there are in the *Boke* a number of jokes—very good jokes—which nevertheless come a little unexpectedly from a lady whose piety and chastity alike were doubtless beyond question. There is, for instance, a sly and mischievous comparison between the qualities required in a horse and those deemed desirable in a woman; both should be '*fair-breasted, fair-haired,* and *easy to be leap'd on.*' And so, taking everything into consideration, we shall probably agree with Dr. Andrew Kippis, who asks (in his *Biographia Britannica*) whether it is likely that 'such a sedate, grave, pious, matron-like lady as the Prioress of a Nunnery' should be also 'one of your romping, roaring hoydens that will be for horsing and hunting after the wildest game in the most giddy company.' 'In that light,' he adds indignantly, 'there appears such a motley masquerade, such an indistinction of petticoat and breeches, such a problem and concorporation of sexes, according to the image that arises out of the several representations of this religious Sportswoman or Virago, that one can scarcely consider it, without thinking Sir Tristram, the old Monkish Forester, and Juliana, the Matron of the Nuns, had united to form John Cleveland's *Canonical Hermaphrodite.*'

However, it doesn't matter very much who Dame Juliana was, or whether she wrote the *Treatyse,* or whether she ever existed at all; it suffices that the book has the morning in it, and that when we read it we can hear across the centuries the same blackbirds singing as those which sing to us when, with rod in hand or without one, we go down to the river in the mayfly-time.

A TREATISE

AND DISCOVRSE OF the Lawes of the Forrest: Wherin is declared not onely those Lawes, as they are now in force, but also the originall *and beginning of Forrestes: And what a Forrest* is in his owne proper nature, and wherein the same doth differ from a Chase, a Park, or a Warren, with all such thinges as are incident or belonging thereunto, with their seuerall proper Tearmes of art: as more at large doth appeare in the Table in the beginning of this Booke.

Also a Treatise of the Purallee, declaring what *Purallee is, how the same first began, what a Pur-*allee man may doe, how he may hunt and vse his owne Purallee, how far he may pursue and follow after his chase, together with the lymits and boundes, aswell of the Forrest, as the Puralley.

Collected and gathered together, aswell out of the Common Lawes and Statutes of this land, As also out of sundry learned auncient Aucthors, and out of the Assises and Iters of Pickring and Lancaster, by IOHN MANWOOD.

AT LONDON

Printed by Thomas Wight and Bonham Norton. 1598.

Cum Priuilegio.

TITLE-PAGE OF MANWOOD'S 'FOREST LAWS'

Chapter 3 *The Greenwood*

CHAUCER's pilgrims kept to the high road, and Dame Juliana's fishermen took the meadow-way down to the river; neither ventured into the woodlands, which were dark places where no birds sang. Only the huntsmen went there when they chased the wild deer; and if you read Manwood's sixteenth-century *Treatise and Discourse of the Lawes of the Forest* you will hear the cry of the hounds and the sound of the horn and the crackling of trampled twigs, but you will find no sunshine and no flowers and no birds singing. You will feel like a trespasser in that dark deep forest; for there broods over it the shadow of the King's Majesty, ever watchful for the safety of the King's deer. 'Hunting in Forrest, Chases, and such like priviledged places of pleasure,' states Manwood, 'is onely for Kings, Princes, and great worthy personages, and not for mean men of mean calling or ambition.' And there are swift and terrible penalties for 'mean men' who are found with blackened face or bloody hand in the King's woodland: the hand that loosed the arrow at the hind shall be cut off, the eyes that looked covetously at the young fawns shall be put out. Because of this, fear lurks always in Manwood's forest—fear of the darkness and of the unseen watchers that dog the steps even of the innocent man who ventures there. When you turn over the musty pages of that old *Treatise and Discourse* (which, incidentally, contain some passages of splendid English prose) you will be keenly aware of this fear and this darkness. Even the stags which start up and crash away through the undergrowth, even the fallow hinds and the soft-eyed little fawns which peep out between the branches—even these are somehow sinister because of their associations; and there broods over all a memory of *Domesday*, of William the Conqueror's great swearing blustering presence, of Rufus's bestial cruelty, and of the swift arrow which sped out of the shadows to avenge it.

There are deep shadows everywhere in this forest of Manwood's, so that one has the feeling that it was in fact a *black* forest: dark deeds were done there, outlaws lay hid there, and the rays of the sun never found their way through the thick branches of the trees. Rosalind's and Touchstone's merry laughter would never have been heard in such a place, Puck would have found no freckled cowslips there, nor Titania's fairies have answered to their sweet names, Peaseblossom, Cobweb, Mustardseed, and Moth. For they are creatures of the greenwood, and the greenwood did not come into being until the Elizabethan sunrise lit the leaves.

The difference between Shakespeare's woods and the older forests is all the difference between light and darkness. William the Conqueror's desolate chases seem as remote from us to-day as do the wolf-haunted tracts of Siberia or the frightening forests of fairy-tale in which Red Riding Hood's grandmother lived. But any familiar glade might be a glade in Arden, and any Warwickshire coppice will serve to remind us of that 'wood near to Athens' which was Athenian only in name.

The explanation of this is not that the forests suddenly changed in character during the sixteenth century, but that men saw them in a new light. That same dazzling sunrise that lit the path to the Indies and Cathay showed the way through the English woodlands too, the bright light splashed into the glades between the oak trees and robbed them of their terrors for the first time, and even the deer-stealer feared no more awful an expression of the royal displeasure than that which manifested itself rather comically in the person of Mr. Justice Shallow.

This all-pervading Elizabethan sunlight drenches the pages of *England's Helicon*, published in 1600, shining honey-coloured, sherry-coloured, through a hundred pastorals:

> My Phyllis hath the morning Sun,
> At first to look upon her;
> And Phyllis hath morn-waking birds,
> Her rising still to honour.

It lights up the little golden crown of Michael Drayton's daffodil that dances on a hill-top in Warwickshire:

> She 's in a frock of Lincoln-green,
> The colour maids delight;
> And never hath her beauty seen
> But through a veil of white.

And it shines upon the lady's-smocks in the meadows by the Avon till Shakespeare sees them 'silver-white' on an April day. Indeed, one might say that not only does it make the woods green for the first time, but it discovers for the first time the humble flowers that lie hid in them. Shakespeare's landscape is familiar to us largely because of the flowers. The lilies and marigolds of some of the Court poets are pretty abstractions;

they might grow anywhere — or nowhere. But there is no mistaking Shakespeare's 'daffodils that come before the swallow dares,' his

> Pale primroses
> That die unmarried ere they can behold
> Bright Phoebus in his strength; a malady
> Most incident to maids.

We have seen them growing: those first shivering daffodils in the fields at Dymock, the milky pallor of the love-sick primroses speckling the brown warrens in the Warwickshire woods. And the flowers that made up Ophelia's fantastic garland, the

> crow-flowers, nettles, daisies, and long purples
> That liberal shepherds give a grosser name,
> But our cold maids do dead men's fingers call them—

we can go and pick such a handful upon any April morning when the spring orchids are out in the damp meadows; we can gather the burdocks, hemlocks, and cuckoo-flowers for mad Lear's weedy crown in any English hedge; while the 'hateful docks, rough thistles, kecksies, burs' in *Henry V* might grow at any familiar stream-side. Indeed, our country-folk still use the word 'kecksies' for the dry hollow stems of the cowbane and the hemlock, and it gives one a pleasant sense of the continuity of country things to find it in Shakespeare. Descriptions of the countryside are never appreciably 'dated.' The ways of society and the fashions of townspeople may change and change again, but the woods and the fields and the men who work in them remain the same through the centuries. The brilliant Elizabethan Court seems as preposterous and distant now as the Court of a fairy princess; the language of Lyly's *Euphues* is as strange-sounding and dated as anything in English; and yet when we read about the countryside in Shakespeare we often feel as if we are reading about last April, with its cuckoos and its cuckoo-flowers.

We have the same feeling about the country contentments of Gervase Markham; fashions don't change in sport, or if they do the changes are slight ones—a matter of breeding longer-legged dogs or lighter horses. And in husbandry too, although the details may alter, although we may use a binder instead of a scythe and an iron plough instead of a wooden one, the essential truths of sowing and reaping, of breeding stock or draining meadows, are not affected by the passage of the years. If we met Gervase Markham in a country inn to-morrow we should find plenty of familiar things to talk about; whereas if we met Leicester or Essex we should not understand a third of their conversation. The witty and elaborate Court idiom which was fashionable in 1590 would seem more strange to us than the quick slang of a Chicago speak-easy; the gossip of that little world in which a man could be thrown into the Tower for an amorous indiscretion and banished for a woman's whim would be comprehensible only to historians; the tale of rivalries and beheadings, of scandals and sonnets, of poets and patronage, of swift fortunes and sudden ruin, would seem to us like a nightmare, a fantasia. Yet Gervase Markham's country talk about ploughing and horses and game would not seem strange at all. We might smile at the phraseology when he told us that a coal-black without any white was always 'a cholerick horse,' partaking 'more of the fire than of the other elements,' but we should understand exactly what he meant, because we know that a black horse is always a jumpy, skittish, temperamental one. And when he warned us, concerning our angling apparel, that it be 'plain and comely, of a dark colour, as Russet, Tawney, or such-like, close to your body, without any new fashioned flashes, or hanging sleeves, waving loose, like sails about you, for they are like blinks, which will ever chase your game from you,' we should most heartily agree, for however much the fashions of men may change, the ways of trout do not change; they are still shyer than hares and sharper-eyed than eagles, in the crystal-clear chalk-stream that runs past the mill.

Chapter 4 — *Spring Morning*

You can go a-Maying in English literature and find there many a sweet spring morning—that songsters' dawn in Chaucer's *Prologue,* full of elvish laughter, those sunny pastorals in *England's Helicon.* You can find dancing daffodils in Michael Drayton, you can pluck hawthorn sprigs in Herrick; but when you come to *The Compleat Angler* your search will be ended, for there is a book that is the whole spring. It has the very air and spirit of those cowslip days, it possesses all the showers and the shadows and the sunshine of May. Indeed, so completely vernal is it that it is almost safe from the anthologists. Elsewhere those scissors-and-paste fellows may snip happily enough, stealing for their delight a bunch of primroses here, a lovers' whisper there, nor greatly caring what other delights they are leaving behind; but surely even the most heartless of them would lay down his scissors when he came to Walton's book, would hesitate to pick and choose bits of it, because he wanted it all. I cannot believe that there is any one who would desire to have it piecemeal. It goes into your pocket whole, unscissored, unabridged; and in your pocket you have all England and all the spring.

Andrew Lang said charmingly that it was 'a book to be marked with flowers, marsh-marigolds and fritillaries, and petals of the yellow iris,' and I do not doubt that its pages have frequently held such pleasant hostages to memory. Apart from the virtues of its good, sound Elizabethan prose, its kindliness, its spring-morning beauty, it has a certain limited practicality as well; and therefore it has probably been read as often by the waterside as in the study. Doubtless it has been used many times for the purpose of storing flies and gut-casts, has fallen into the water and been rescued with the landing-net, has shared the fishing-basket with a brace of trout or chub. These adventures make it unique as a book, just as angling, which is 'somewhat like poetry,' is unique as a sport. Hunting, if we except the erudition of Peter Beckford and the sweet wistfulness of Mr. Sassoon's *Foxhunting Man,* has always been associated with a sort of hearty unliterariness; shooting, apart from some charming essays by Mr. Eric Parker and the *Punch* lyrics of Mr. Patrick Chalmers, has produced nothing very memorable either in poetry or prose. It is left to angling, the queerest sport that man ever devised, to flirt with the things of the mind and to give birth, astonishingly, to this delicious piece of riverside literature, in which the very may-flies come alive and go dancing over the eddies, in which there are English flowers and meadows, there are cowslips, there is May.

Yet all anglers are not so sensitive. The only contemporary criticism of Walton's book which we may still read is contained in a work called *Northern Memoirs,* written by Richard Franck, himself a fisherman. This Franck was a trooper of Cromwell's, a Northerner, a slightly pedantic fellow, and probably a sour one; for who could ride with men who possessed such names as Praise-god Barebones and still keep a merry face? At any rate, Franck had nothing but contempt for *The Compleat Angler.* He called it an 'indigested octavo,' accused Walton of plagiarism, and hinted that he knew very little about angling:

'He stuffs his book with morals from Dubravius and others, not giving us one precedent of his own experiments, except otherwise where he prefers the trencher to the trolling-rod; he lays the stress of his arguments upon other men's observations, wherewith he stuffs his indigested octavo; so brings himself under the angler's censure, and the common calamity of a plagiary, to be pitied (poor man) for his loss of time, in scribbling and transcribing other men's notions. These are the drones that rob the hive, yet flatter the bees that bring them honey.'

Now the temper of Cromwell's men was so dismal—or the historians have made it appear so—that it would really be surprising if one of them saw any beauty in anything; they preferred to cast their eyes downward, looking cheerlessly for hell-fire. And perhaps this is the reason why Franck failed to notice the sunshine in Walton's book, and saw only the inaccuracy and the superstition. Yet Franck was himself an extremely good writer and one would expect him to appreciate Walton's prose even if he did not admire his methods of angling; for he had the right feeling for words, had Captain Richard Franck, and he could write with a fine floridity of poachers: 'What, are these canabals, or murdering moss-troopers, to surprise fish by the engine of firelight? Such dark conspirators sprung from the mines in Florida, Fawks, or Cataline; or some infernal incubus.' Surely he was capable of appreciating Walton's craftsmanship with the pen, if not with the fishing-rod? However, we must remember that Walton was on the side of the King. If Franck was not prejudiced, at least he had good cause to be so. On the one occasion when these two met, at Stafford, and Walton 'huffed away' because Franck teased him about one of his pet theories (that pikes were bred out of pickerel-weed), there was possibly another and a stronger reason for disagreement, if Walton happened to mention King Charles. . . .

Nevertheless—though this is heresy—I am inclined to believe that Walton was not a very expert fisherman after all. Franck was; he caught salmon and trout in the Esk, and in the swift, dangerous northern streams. Old Izaak's methods were antiquated even for those times; he had probably never used a reel, and could not even describe one, though he got out of the difficulty by a pleasing piece of humbug: 'Some use a wheel about the middle of their rod, or near their hand, which is to be observed better by seeing one of them than by a large demonstration of words.' Moreover, he knew nothing at all about salmon (and yet wrote a nonsensical chapter about them), he had probably never wielded a fly-rod, and he stole his list of flies from his mysterious predecessor, Dame Juliana Berners. But what must have shocked Franck most of all was Walton's concern with the small fry, the trivial side-lines of fishing. Like an urchin with a bent pin, he was content to spend long afternoons fishing for little dace and gudgeon in the Shawford Brook; to Franck he must have seemed an amateur indeed! Never to have felt the first thrilling terrible rush of a salmon in a swift river! Never to have raced downstream praying that the line might hold while a clean-run fish leaped again and again at the end of it! And yet boldly to assert that gudgeons and bleaks and daddy-ruffs were 'excellent fish' and to be content to angle for them! No wonder Franck was contemptuous. It is very hard, when you have once fished for salmon, to believe that anything else is worth fishing for; you have to be something of a poet, or a whimsical fellow like the late Hugh Sheringham. I, who am neither, have been guilty these last two years of making a solemn vow, in the train between Perth and Crewe, that never again would I wet a line except in the cause of salmon and trout. I have broken it each year, at the request of a cousin who wanted company on an expedition to a muddy pond where dwelt some peculiarly nauseous pike; but that was charity to my cousin rather than partiality for pike. In spirit I am a purist still; and if you call me a snob I must remind you that even kindly Andrew Lang remarked that 'a bait-fisher *may* be a good man, as Izaak was, but it is easier for a camel to pass through the eye of a needle.'

Franck probably held the same opinion. Remember also that he was a Parliament man, unlikely to be well-disposed towards a Royalist; that he was a Puritan [1]—and raffish Charles Cotton had contributed a chapter to *The Compleat Angler*; that he was a practical-minded person, whereas Izaak was highly superstitious; and finally that he did not understand that angling was 'somewhat like poetry'—and, making these allowances, perhaps we can excuse him for being unmoved by Izaak's May morning, perhaps we can even forgive his unkind words about the 'indigested octavo.'

Moreover, Izaak's credulity was sufficient to try the patience of any hard-headed, common-sensical person. He stuffed his book with all sorts of curious beliefs, copied without question from Pliny and Gesner and Gerard, and from such strange sources as Du Bartas, Lobel, Camden, and Dubravius. Thus, caterpillars 'have their birth, or being, from a dew that in the spring falls upon the leaves of trees'; the salamander also is born 'without Venus' deed' of 'the cold humour'; the firefly of the fire; barnacles of wrecked ships; young goslings of the sun's heat; eels of 'corruption of the earth'; pike, of course, of pickerel-weed. Hares change their sex every year; salmon,

[1] Franck subsequently went to America, where he wrote a very wild and strange work called *The Admirable and Indefatigable Adventures of Nine Pious Pilgrims,* in which one of the pilgrims catches a trout!

remaining in fresh water beyond their accustomed season, turn into trout; frogs change to slime in winter, and back to frogs in the summer, are venomous, and should be handled with care. And so on. Izaak even quotes one 'Gasper Peucerus, a learned physician,' as telling 'of a people that once a year turned into wolves,' and he does not quarrel with the statement, but even prints it with approval, as an example that there are more things in heaven and earth than are dreamed of in man's philosophy.

The truth of the matter is that Izaak had an enormous respect for learned authority. Give him plenty of footnotes, so to speak, and he 'd believe anything. There are men as wise as he who are taken in like that to-day, so we can hardly blame him. And we find that in the actual practice of his angling, in matters that came within his own experience, he was too shrewd to be very credulous. In fact, when he is told that a hundred and sixty minnows have been found in the belly of a trout, he permits himself the unworthy suspicion that the miller who gave the fish to his friend 'had forced them down his throat after he had taken him.' The miller, poor man, was no 'learned physician,' and couldn't dazzle Izaak with wise-sounding quotations from the unfamiliar Latin!

Nevertheless, Izaak has a brief flirtation with

magic oils ('Dissolve gum of ivy in oil of spike, and therewith anoint your bait'), and he has been told that 'any bait anointed with the marrow of the thigh-bone of a heron is a great temptation to any fish.' He is careful to add, however, that 'these have not been tried by me, but told me by a friend of note, that pretended to do me a courtesy.' One detects a certain faint scepticism here; and perhaps, too, a little scorn, for Izaak was no pot-hunter and I do not think it would have greatly pleased him to have taken fish by the aid of such witch-doctors' potions as these, nor with such gruesome mixtures as 'man's fat, cat's fat, mummy finely powdered, and grave earth,' nor with 'the Bones and Skull of a Dead-man, at the opening of a Grave'—which are some of the ingredients contained in a charming recipe printed in *The Angler's Vade Mecum*, a later book than Walton's.

In fact, although he fished for samlets and 'caught twenty or forty at a standing,' although he was guilty of trimmering for pike—both of which offences would land him in court to-day—he was, by the standards of his time, a very fair fisherman, and never a greedy one. Angling, for him, was not a matter for record-making or for competition, and heaven knows what he would say if he could see a modern fishing-match, organized by some such body as the Birmingham Anglers' Society, and started, like a race, by the shot of a pistol. . . . He lived in a wiser age, and was spared such horrible exhibitions—luckily for us, for no *Compleat Angler* is likely to be born out of the Birmingham sport. No: in Izaak's case angling was merely an excuse to be at the riverside, and that is what it should be: at once an art, a sport, an adventure, and an essay in quietude. One cannot well imagine these fishing-match heretics thinking thus of the meadows: 'That they were too pleasant to be looked on, but only on holy-days'; they prefer to strew them with orange-peel and paper bags! Nor can one fancy them beguiling themselves with 'that smooth song which was made by Kit Marlowe, and an answer to it which was made by Sir Walter Raleigh, in his younger days'; they are too much concerned with the odds—for, strange though it sounds, these Birmingham men have bookmakers at their competitions, and they back themselves to win fifty or a hundred pounds if they should chance to catch more seven-inch sprats than their fellows. *O tempora! O mores!* Izaak wrote sadly: 'Only we who have lived these last twenty years are certain that money has been able to do much mischief,' and one feels that the sentence might almost have been written to-day. But certainly

Izaak never contemplated that his gudgeon-catching would be organized into a matter for betting.

It is rather strange that so quiet a harvest as *The Compleat Angler* should have come out of such unquiet times. While Izaak was planning and writing his book, England was at Civil War. In Scotland Montrose raised the Highlands for his King and lost gallantly to Leslie at Philliphaugh, and in the south Edgehill, Marston Moor, Naseby, Newark, and Colchester sealed the fate of Charles. On more than one of his fishing days, Izaak must have heard the clatter of hoofs on the bridge and left his float unwatched while he cheered the plumed cavaliers or frowned at those other soldiers, the queer sour fellows who sang hymns and fought for Parliament. But the hymn-singers won, and Charles, condemned a murderer and a traitor, lost his head and gained his martyrdom.

Four years later, when Cromwell was unmaking one parliament and making another, a parliament of saints with weird names, Izaak's undistinguished-looking eighteen-penny octavo first saw light in a troubled world. Within the next twelve years, which witnessed the Restoration, the Plague, the Fire of London, and the Dutch raid on the Medway, it ran through five editions; so even in those stirring times the may-fly did not forget to come out, and 'anglers, honest men,' still had leisure to concern themselves with it. Izaak himself must have seen many strange events, but he had not the inquisitiveness of Pepys, and he preferred fishing to sightseeing. Perhaps, however, on the glorious night when the King came into his own again he forgot his fishing and his grave scholarship for a few hours and, casting aside his piety, took part in the most magnificent debauch in England's history. Andrew Lang, whom I must quote for a third time, remarks pleasantly: 'If Izaak were so eccentric as to go to bed sober on that glorious twenty-ninth of May, I greatly misjudge him.' I echo that kindly sentiment, and add the guess that his roystering young friend, Charles Cotton, called for him and took him out mafficking, and brought him home very drunk indeed. Next day the may-fly would be up, and they could cool their heads at the riverside!

Izaak was in London during the Plague year, and he may also have seen the Fire; but he did not write any account of these things and went quietly on with his work, collaborating with Cotton in the revised *Compleat Angler* and finishing his *Lives.* If he had been a diarist like Pepys, a student of the ways of men instead of the ways of fish, he would have been a profitable source to the historians; for he lived during five reigns—Elizabeth, James I, Charles I, the Commonwealth, and

Charles II. He was born at Stafford in 1593 and he died in December 1683 at the very remarkable age—for his time—of ninety. He lived for the most part in London, and practised the trade of an ironmonger; and it is a curious thing that in small towns to-day it is generally the ironmonger who sells rods and lines and hooks for fishing. For all we know Izaak may have sold such implements himself in his younger days, and so set a fashion in the trade.

He should really have been a cleric; he had a simple faith, unshaken by the speculations of his age, and in a country parsonage (with a mile of river as part of the glebe!) he would have been as happy as the day was long. His simplicity in religious matters was altogether delightful, and somewhat surprising in the age of such men as Donne. Writing of Dr. Nowel, another Dean of Saint Paul's, he expresses his own faith perfectly: 'And the good old man, though he was very learned, yet knowing that God leads us not to Heaven by many, nor by hard questions, made that good, plain, unperplexed Catechism which is printed with our good old Service-book.' Mark that '*though he was very learned.*' Izaak always kept his respect for scholarship, but said in effect: 'I am a poor simple man, and I do not understand intricate things; you are wise and you may speculate as much as you like so long as you leave me a plain, simple faith which is within my understanding.' His ignorance was the sort of ignorance which is very, very wise. The soap-box orators of to-day would do well to imitate it.

It is characteristic of Izaak's religious simplicity that he takes great pains to seek commendation of his favourite sport in the Scriptures. He zealously hunts through the Bible for fish-hooks, and is almost pathetically pleased when he imagines he finds them. 'Let me tell you,' he declares, 'that in the Scripture, angling is always taken in the best sense.' He is encouraged by the discovery that 'God is said to have spoken to a fish, but never to a beast.' It is fortunate that he did not know that Jonah's whale was a mammal!

He gives a long list of divines who have found their pleasure in angling. 'Let me add this more,' he writes contentedly. 'He that views the ancient Ecclesiastical Canons, shall find hunting to be forbidden to clergymen, as being a turbulent, toilsome, perplexing recreation; and shall find Angling allowed to clergymen, as being a harmless recreation, a recreation that invites them to contemplation and quietness.'

To find this authority must have pleased him greatly. He hated perplexing things, and he delighted in the company of the clergy. Circumstances prevented him from taking orders himself, but he did the best he could by marrying episcopally. His wife, Rachel Floud, was a descendant of Cranmer, and a friend of the family of Hooker. Already Izaak could claim for friends such famous divines as John Donne, Dr. King, Hales of Eton, and Sir Henry Wotton. In such ecclesiastical company he was always happy; and very good company it must have been. Wotton was himself an angler, and, what was more, a fly-fisher; though it is not recorded that he ever converted Izaak from his wretched floats and worms to the more honourable pastime. Wotton, and Donne too, had the pleasant hobby of telling ghost-stories, which they shared with Izaak. One can imagine that the Dean of Saint Paul's, in his grim later days, was very good at making his hearers' flesh creep! He and Izaak had something else in common which may have had a lot to do with their close friendship. They shared, not only a present piety, but a somewhat impious past. Donne's young days and nights had been full of fair ladies; and even quiet old Izaak, we are told, had been 'a very sweet poet in his youth, and more than all in matters of love.' [1] Both preacher and angler had reformed; they had given up their love-lyrics with the ladies who had

[1] In a lost MS. mentioned by Sir Harris Nicolas.

inspired them, and while Donne preached thunderous sermons Izaak concerned himself with country delights. Nevertheless, the reformed rake rarely loses a queer lurking pride in his previous rakishness, and perhaps these two pious old gentlemen occasionally forgot their gravity as they sat before the fire on a winter's night, and unbent slightly as the hour grew late. 'In my young days, you know . . .' Izaak would say, smiling faintly at the memory. 'In mine . . .' Donne would echo. Then Izaak—who must have known the poem by heart—would quote impishly from the earlier, and most unclerical, works of the divine:

> I scarce believe my love to be so pure
> As I had thought it was. . . .

And Donne would shake his head, and look slightly uncomfortable, and reprove Izaak's mischief with a piece of scholarship. '*Amare et sapere vix deo conceditur.*' Then Izaak, awed as ever by the Latin, would change the subject, and tell a ghost-story.

Charles Cotton was a later friend of Izaak's. He belonged more to the Court than to the countryside, but he wrote one poem that seems to contain all the wonder and surprise of a man who sees green fields for the first time. Perhaps it is less a poem than an exclamation, a *cri de cœur*; there is a sort of breathless amazement about it, and I am prepared to swear that it came into his head as he stood at a Derbyshire riverside one morning in May:

> Good God! how sweet are all things here!
> How beautiful the fields appear!
> How cleanly do we feed and lie!
> Lord! What good hours do we keep!
> How quietly we sleep!
> What peace! What unanimity!
> How innocent from the lewd fashion
> Is all our bus'ness, all our conversation!

Cotton knew Lovelace and Suckling, wrote wittily, drank heavily, and got himself into debt. But he was a fisherman and a Royalist, and that was enough for Izaak; the two collaborated, and there is no doubt that the younger was the better angler. Mr. Eric Taverner has said that 'Walton without Cotton is like good manners without meat'; and that is quite true. (Good manners, however, may often excuse a bad meal.) At any rate, Cotton's very practical treatise on fly-fishing was added to the new edition of *The Compleat Angler*, and his initials were joined with Izaak's in the fishing-house which they built on the Dove. This was in 1676. Strange times, when England was still a little light-headed. Izaak must have been sadly puzzled by some of the tales which reached him of the goings-on at Court. Sir

Charles Sedley, Lord Buckhurst, and one Sir Thomas Ogle had disgraced themselves at a time when disgrace was difficult to achieve by standing stark-naked on a balcony and preaching mock sermons to the crowd. Izaak, disapproving of 'Scripture jests and lascivious jests,' would surely have been shocked at this. Rochester and Etheredge, meanwhile, were piling excess upon excess in a desperate effort to disprove that the last extremity of vice was merely boredom. Charles himself was busy with Moll Davis and already, perhaps, had his eye on Nell Gwynne, who was playing at the King's House. If Izaak saw her there he must have fallen in love with her, for she had the freshness of his own prose. Among the tired pleasure-seekers of the Restoration she must have seemed very gay and simple, an English primrose among hot-house flowers.

But these were not really Izaak's times. Dryden was writing wicked, witty verse ('the strong lines that are now in fashion in this critical age'); England was ready for the studied artifice of Pope. Izaak was in spirit an Elizabethan, and he had more in common with Michael Drayton, an earlier friend, than with Cotton's queer crew. The young bucks must have sorely tried his charity. In his book he had written: 'I do seriously approve of that saying of yours, that you have rather be a civil, well-governed, well-grounded, temperate poor angler, than a drunken lord: *but I hope there is none such.*' It would be a pious hope in Restoration times! There were precious few lords who were ever sober. Their best excuse is that they seem to have been wittiest when drunk, and that now and then they wrote good verses; but somehow they had lost the 'spring-morning feeling,' if I may so express it, which Walton and the Elizabethans had. They had ceased to feel that the world was wide. They had lost the spirit of setting forth on an adventure. Perhaps they had had too much adventure. Their parties had gone on too long.

There is a tale told [1] of a dance given by Charles to the Prince of Neuberg in Saint James's Park, which went on all night and into the dawn, and finished as a fishing-party on the landing-stage at Hampton Court. Charles was a keen fisherman, though a very unskilful one. All he caught was a minnow, and he became bored and sauntered away. Nell (who was then at the height of her success) saw the chance of the sort of joke she loved. When the King returned he noticed that his rod was bending bravely. 'Look, Charles, look!' cried Nell. 'At last you really have a catch!' Charles drew in his line and landed—a

[1] Clifford Bax, *Pretty Witty Nell.*

handful of dried smelts! 'What is there strange in that?' asked Nell. 'Subjects should catch their fish alive, but a king should find his ready cooked!'

I wonder if Izaak would have appreciated the jest. Perhaps it was not quite in his manner. He liked to sleep well o' nights and to be fresh when he went down to the river in the morning. But he was above all a kindly man, and for all his piety he was never censorious. Nell could not have failed to captivate him; and for my part I hope that he laughed a little if he were told of the strange fishing that happened that day at Hampton Court.

This incident—perhaps apocryphal—occurred in 1672. *The Compleat Angler* was still selling, for a new edition was published four years later; but that was the last until 1750, when Johnson suggested to Moses Brown that he should bring it out 'with improvements.'

The gap is a big one. England had forgotten country delights, and was not to rediscover them till near the time of Wordsworth. It is difficult to believe that there were no 'anglers, honest men' who went down to the river in those years; but there must have been few, or surely Izaak's little book would not have remained out of print for so long.

As for Izaak himself, he lived for seventeen years after his revised edition was published. In 1683 he wrote his will, in the ninetieth year of his age and in perfect memory, 'for which praised be God.' Even at the last his kindliness did not desert him; for though he professed the Anglican faith he stoutly affirmed his 'very long and very trew friendship for some of the Roman Church.' He was no bigot! He declared that his estate had been acquired 'neither by falsehood or flattery or the extreme crewelty of the law.' He bequeathed gifts to the poor of Stafford, a ring to the Bishop of Winchester, and ten pounds to his 'old friend, Mr. Robert Marriott,' who had published the first editions of *The Compleat Angler*.

It has always been believed that he was a kindly man, and an exceptionally patient one, but his will provides the final proof. He died in peace with his publisher, and even left him some money.

ROBERT HERRICK

Chapter 5 *Twilight in Devon*

GOODNESS knows how Master Robert Herrick creeps into this book. He was born and bred a Londoner, and he regarded his time spent in the country as a hated exile. Moreover, his love for the countryside was of the vicarious kind: he liked it at a distance, but he hated its muddy proximity. He enjoyed the daffodils but not the dirt, the snowdrops but not the snow. Yet perhaps he has a place here nevertheless, and that is the place of a convert; for there came a time, I think, in his old age, when he ceased to be an alien in the unfriendly Devon countryside, when London called him no longer, and when he grew to accept the muddy lanes as part of the landscape which he rather surprisingly loved.

He was a contemporary of Walton's and, like

Walton, he had more kinship with the Elizabethans than with the writers of his own time. His work had the spirit of noonday at a time when England seemed to be in twilight. The sunset had come when the greatest queen that England had ever known fell to the floor in her palace at Richmond and lay there, tragically grotesque, with her finger in her mouth; the blazing glory ended then, but the sunset was a slow, reluctant one with a flickering afterglow. Into this strange light that never was on sea or land the Last Elizabethan, Sir Walter Ralegh grown old and reckless, sailed out in search of his El Dorado; and at home, in the Apollo Room at the Old Devil Tavern, the tremendous form of Ben Jonson sought to warm itself in the last rays. He must have felt the night creeping on, shivered at the chilly shades that were so soon to quench the glory of Elizabethan poetry, for the poets were dying one by one—Rob Greene and Tom Nash and Francis Beaumont, and Kit Marlowe who was the morning star of that bright galaxy—all were dead, and the greatest poet the world had ever heard had hid himself at Stratford-on-Avon in Warwickshire and was sulking there, bored with himself, bored with living, bored with everything except the magical music of words. Ah, 'twas a chilly time, thought old Ben Jonson, a twilight ghost-haunted, and the best remedies against ghosts were plenty of sack and plenty of lively company. So Ben—Ben of the mountainous belly, who looked rather like a tub of sack himself—drank prodigiously in the Apollo Room and gathered about him a little group of new young poets who were called the Tribe of Ben. They were witty enough, and scholarly enough, and perhaps, when Ben had drunk an exceptionally large quantity of the excellent sherris, he might bring himself to believe that some of them were fit to lick the boots of Kit Marlowe, who had died when the world was young. Most of them are half-forgotten now. There was young Randolph, there were Carew, Mayne, Howell, and a dozen more; and they were joined about the year 1620 by Robert Herrick, who had just finished his education at Cambridge University.

Robert Herrick at this time was a very gay young man, he had written a good deal of poetry already, he had a taste for the sack and an eye for the ladies, so he thought he would tarry in London for a little, while he made up his mind whether the profession of the Law or that of the Church was best suited to his talents. It took him nine years to decide; and during those nine years he sat at the feet of Ben Jonson, went frequently to the play, wrote innumerable pretty verses to innumerable pretty mistresses, and celebrated the sack which old Simon

Wadloe the landlord looked after so carefully. 'We have spent our time,' he boasted afterwards (in rather jolly but slightly bombastic verses):

> We have spent our time,
> Both from the morning to the evening chime . . .
> With flame and rapture; drinking to the odd
> Number of nine, which makes us full with God,
> And in that mystic frenzy we have hurled
> (As with a tempest) Nature through the world. . . .

And so on. Thus the Tribe of Ben; and Robert Herrick had nine years of them until, on a day in 1629, he suddenly came to the conclusion that he must concern himself with things of even greater moment than sherris-sack, and, not without a reluctant look back at his field of wild oats so greenly growing, he took Holy Orders and went into a sort of voluntary exile as the parish priest of Dean Prior near Totnes town in Devon.

Dean Prior is a very pleasant place. Between the wooded coombes there the bright River Dean runs down to join the Dart at Buckfastleigh; not sixteen miles away lies Plymouth, and the blue Devon sea. But all the same it would be very dishonest to pretend that the new incumbent was happy, at first, with his country parsonage and his charge of five hundred country souls. His heart ached for London Town, for the company of men who could appreciate a Latin epigram, for Ben

Jonson's great gusty laughter, for poetry, and for ladies. He was a thoroughly rebellious parson. He had written very prettily of the pastoral scene, of the daffodils and the primroses and the violets, but goodness! how very unpleasant was the pastoral scene in winter, with mud in the lanes up to your horse's hocks, and a bitter wind off the moors curling the snowflakes into your face! Poor Parson Herrick hated it, and, in the long winter evenings when he was confined to his house, he sat down and sent flowing from his quill another spate of poems—poems in which he sighed for London, poems in which he cursed Devonshire, rough epigrams (like Martial at his worst) in which he satirized his parishioners without mercy, and, for contrast, neatly turned compliments to all those pretty ladies who existed now, alas! only in memory:

I have lost, and lately, these
Many dainty Mistresses:
Stately Julia, prime of all;
Sappho next, a principal;
Smooth Anthea, for a skin
White, and Heaven-like Chrystalline;
Sweet Electra, and the choice
Myrha, for the Lute and Voice;
Next Corinna, for her wit,
And the graceful use of it;
With Perilla: All are gone;
Only Herrick 's left alone.

Of course we cannot wholly believe that all these virtuous ladies had any existence whatever outside Herrick's imagination. Goddesses walked on earth no more frequently in 1630 than they do to-day; and it is dreadfully probable that sweet Electra was really a serving-wench at the 'Old Devil,' and stately Julia an orange-seller at the Globe Theatre, and smooth Anthea a successor to Doll Tearsheet at Mistress Quickly's house in Bread Street! But anyhow poor Herrick missed them, and here in Devon the only company he had about his household was a goose, a cock and a hen, a tame lamb, a cat, a spaniel, a pet pig which he had taught to drink out of a tankard, and last but not least, his ancient maid Prudence Baldwin. And excellent woman though Prue was (Herrick didn't forget to praise her domestic virtues in verse), she wasn't, I am afraid, very much to look at, and her presence about the place must have been a very poor substitute for that of Sylvia, Sappho, Electra, Dianeme, and all the rest of the Graces.

No doubt the Devonshire exile seemed quite endless, and Herrick could see no hope of escape from it until he should die. But eventually he did escape, though not of his own will. In January 1649 King Charles the First, whom some call saint and martyr, died upon the scaffold with almost incredible gallantry, and a black cloud descended upon England in the shape of Oliver Cromwell. Now Parson Herrick was, as you may imagine, very much of a Royalist; and a Royalist he would continue, let all the dismal praying crew go hang. Consequently he was politely but firmly removed from his living, and he went very cheerfully to London, pausing on his way only to write a most disagreeable farewell to the county of his adoption:

> A people currish; churlish as the seas;
> And rude (almost) as rudest Savages;
> With whom I did, and may re-sojourn, when
> Rocks turn to rivers, rivers turn to men.

That was very uncharitable of Master Herrick; and no doubt he was properly punished for it by the discovery that London, his beloved city, was not the London he had known any more. Ben Jonson was dead, and the Apollo Room was peopled only by ghosts. The sun had set upon the Elizabethans at last. Burbage as Hamlet no longer told the world that it was mad; Ned Alleyn as Romeo no longer told Juliet in her balcony that two of the fairest stars in all the heaven were not comparable with her eyes. The Globe Theatre was shut, and there were no more plays.

In this strange, sad, unfamiliar London Herrick

lived for some fifteen years, supported chiefly by his friends. During this time he published a collection of his poems under the pleasant title *Hesperides*; and the publication of such merry, wanton verses must have seemed like a rather gallant gesture—as if he offered them as a gift to the Cavaliers who were so out of fashion in those gloomy days. The book is full of ladies, of Sappho, Sylvia, Electra, and all those ethereal beauties of Herrick's younger days, but it is also crowded with flowers and with simple country delights, and with the *lares et penates* of a countryman's household. Pansies and primroses, wassails and wedding-cakes, jostle strangely, and not altogether incongruously, with the lips, breasts, thighs and those demesnes which Mercutio conjured by, of unnumbered goddesses. 'I sing,' declared Herrick in his apology:

of Brooks, of Blossoms, Birds, and Bowers:
Of April, May, of June and July Flowers.
I sing of Maypoles, Hock-carts, Wassails, Wakes,
Of Bridegrooms, Brides, and of their Bridal Cakes.
I write of Youth, of Love, and have access
By these, to sing of cleanly Wantonness.
I sing of Dews, of Rains, and piece by piece
Of Balm, of Oil, of Spice, and Ambergris.
I sing of Time's Transhifting; and I write
How Roses first came Red, and Lilies White.

I write of Groves, of Twilights, and I sing
The Court of Mab and of the Fairy-king.
I write of Hell; I sing (and ever shall)
Of Heaven, and hope to have it after all.

That little catalogue would qualify him, I think, for a place in a book about Country Men, even if two of his poems, *Corinna's Going a-Maying* and *Night-piece to Julia,* were not among the loveliest pastorals in the language, the one wet and shining with the morning dew, the other bright with glow-worm lamps and starlight in a country lane.

Of course it may be said, and fairly, that Herrick's countryside was too idyllic to be true; that it was a Londoner's countryside, viewed from afar. It belongs more to Oberon and Titania than to stern reality; it is a fair-weather landscape, peopled by fancies and blest with an eternal spring. Even the flowers assume personalities, like the pansies in the poem *How Pansies or Heart's-ease came first,* which begins so charmingly: 'Frolick virgins once these were, Overloving, living here . . .'; or like the primroses filled with morning dew whom Herrick asks, 'Why do ye weep, sweet Babes?' and bids them:

Speak, whimp'ring Younglings, and make known
The reason why
Ye droop and weep;
Is it for want of sleep?
Or childish lullabie?

Or that ye have not seen as yet
The Violet?
Or brought a kiss
From that Sweet-heart to this?

Countrymen don't think of flowers like this; and it is arguable that Herrick's primroses belong to fairyland rather than to English hedgerows—that one can pick them with the dew on them, and yet not get one's feet wet. One feels, perhaps unjustly, that Herrick would have hated getting his feet wet. Nevertheless, there are moments in his book when the orchards of the Hesperides seem very like the orchards of Devonshire; when Master Herrick suddenly forgets that he is a Londoner, forgets even that he is a fanciful fellow sojourning in the realm of Oberon. Such a moment is that when he comforts himself for his loss of city pleasures:

Yet can thy humble roof maintain a choir
Of singing crickets by the fire,
And the brisk mouse may feed herself with crumbs
Till that the green-eyed kitling comes.

(I love that 'green-eyed kitling'!) Or such another is that when he writes a whole poem about some trifling act of cookery, or praises good Mistress Prue, or describes the rough merry play of his men and maids at maypole-time. There are times, in fact, when one may believe that the

Cockney was converted; and colour is lent to this belief by the fact that he returned to his parsonage. In 1660 the black pall lifted, the King came into his own, and Robert Herrick was restored to his living two years later. Without undue delay and as far as we know without much regret, he went back to Dean Prior, and in spite of his previous bad temper I think he was glad to be back, and that his country-folk were not sorry to see him. Now they would be able to have harvest festivals again, and dancing round the maypole, and the services in the little church would be a good deal merrier, even if parson *did* sometimes curse them roundly from the pulpit. But soon (I believe) they found that parson had mellowed as he had grown old. He might have a fierce and turbulent mood at times, as when he threw his sermon at a member of the congregation who was apparently asleep; or as on that dreadful occasion when somebody brought a squealing pig into the church at harvest festival. But those were just incidents; for he had begun to love his country people, almost against his will, and the conversion of Robert Herrick was complete. Of late the sharp, Martial-like epigrams had come rarely from his pen, and instead he had written marriage greetings comparable with those of Catullus, he had celebrated country cakes and cream and the maypole dance and the pleasant folly of the lasses and lads going a-Maying. Had he not counselled his maidens, 'Gather ye Rose-buds while ye may,' smiling and shaking his head at the dear foolishness of their springtime ? And had he not bidden Corinna spend not too long over her prayers on a May morning, that she might take part in that festival which was older than any Devon countryman's memory ?

It is pleasant to picture him sitting outside his little vicarage on that blue May-day, with his book open upon his knees, scribbling a line now and then as he watches his young people coming back from the may-gathering. The whitethorn has made great snowdrifts in the coombes, and the boys and girls are bringing home armfuls of it, great snowy bunches with which they decorate the porches of the houses. They bring sycamore, too, so that the village street is as green as a park. There is a bunch and a bough for the vicarage door, and a greeting for the vicar from the young folks who bring them. Then they go off, pair by pair, pair by pair, and old Herrick watches them go. He 'll close one eye, perhaps he 'll have to close both eyes, to some of to-day's happenings:

> Many a green gown has been given,
> Many a kiss, both odd and even . . .
> Many a jest told of the keys betraying
> This night, and locks pickt . . .

Well, well. . . . Some would call this a pagan festival, some good Christians would try to put it down. Be hanged to such sour-faced spoil-sports! Let the lasses and lads have their fun; old Herrick doesn't mind—though it 's fortunate, perhaps, that everybody who reads his verses will not know the true meaning of 'giving a green gown' to a maid, nor the full significance of the old country jest about locks and keys. . . . 'I too,' thinks Herrick, 'I too was young once!' and he slowly turns over the pages of his book. Surely there were never so many kisses given and taken within a few printed pages as there are here! Never so much sweet dalliance, never so many light and lovely ladies! Ah well, all that 's over now. . . .

Old Herrick looks across the coombe at the green hill-side beyond, up which he can see his young people going in pairs, arm in arm. Bless them. He smiles and takes up his pen and writes for as long as he can see; and then the slow, soft twilight comes down over the coombe, and blurs the forms of the lovers who go among the sweet-smelling, moth-haunted may-bushes, and the shape of the grey straggly vicarage, and the figure of the old fellow outside it, who has become a countryman at last.

Chapter 6 *Another Parsonage*

JOGGING down the deep-cut lanes, rattling over the hard ruts in summer, splashing through the mud in rainy seasons, straining and heaving through the snowdrifts in winter-time, His Majesty's Mail (some hundred years after the death of Robert Herrick) brought Parson White's correspondence to Selborne and carried his own letters away. He must be a very busy and a very learned man, this country vicar—although his homilies from the pulpit were as dull as ditchwater and as long as a summer noon; for there were always plenty of packets for him—letters addressed in the cramped scholarly hand, letters that bore an academic air, crested letters from English country houses and weirdly-franked communications from foreign parts. There was also a great multitude of parcels. Some of these parcels, from their shape and size, evidently contained books—heavy, leather-bound Latin tomes such as those which darkly lined the study at 'The Wakes'; Parson White was buying more wisdom from London Town! But there were other parcels whose sizes and shapes were diverse and unusual, and whose contents could not possibly be guessed by the man who carried the mail up to the vicar's house. Occasionally a torn corner of their covering would invite an inquisitive peep, and the peep would be rewarded by a glimpse of—feathers or fur! And now and then there would be disquieting evidence that the package contained crawling things. And on hot summer days there would perhaps be a hint to the nose that all was not well with the contents of the package. The maidservant would avert her head as she accepted it at the door. A rare specimen, insufficiently cured, had taken a few days too long in travelling from Mr. Thomas Pennant's house in Flintshire. . . .

Jogging away down the deep-cut lanes, His Majesty's Mail carried back Gilbert White's replies to his numerous correspondents. There were letters to Mr. Pennant (and a parcel for Mr. Pennant too, containing a dead harvest-mouse for his learned consideration); letters to the Honourable Daines Barrington, who had retired from the judicial bench to devote himself to philosophical studies; and more letters, addressed in that rather sprawling handwriting, to the parson's brother at Gibraltar, to Mr. William Markwick, the erudite author of several communications to the Linnean Society, to Dr. John Aiken, and to Mr. Robert Marsham, F.R.S., of Stratton Strawless, Norfolk.

Into the bag they went, with all the other packets and packages which the mail had collected along its route—with documents for London lawyers, with love-letters from Hampshire girls to their soldier-lovers who were fighting in America, with all the trivial greetings and condolences and domestic news which the post bears daily from village to village and town to town. All those other letters must surely be forgotten now; for how frail and impermanent is a good wish or a scrap of news written down on a sheet of note-paper and sent to a friend! Even those love-letters, so ardent, so burning-bright—how rarely they outlive the brief passion which prompted them! Ink fades, as if to prove Love's sure mortality; paper grows yellow, curls up at the edges, becomes brittle and falls to pieces—if, indeed, the fire or the dust-heap have not claimed it first. The good wishes die with their donors, the news ceases to be news and disappears.

But the letters which Parson White wrote to his friends somehow escaped the common fate. In this they were fortunate indeed, because their tone was so quiet and their matter so apparently trivial that they might easily have vanished with all those others which shared their journey in the Hampshire mailbag. They seem, as it were, to have whispered their way into immortality; for they tell of nothing more important than the songs of birds and the changes of the weather and the dates when the flowers came out in a vicar's garden. No historian would bother his head with them for a moment; for they make no mention of the important events which were happening at the time when they were written. While Gilbert White was communicating to Mr. Thomas Pennant his new and ingenious theory of the origin of the domestic pigeon, and corresponding with the Honourable Daines Barrington upon the vexed question of where swallows went in the winter, the world was passing through a period of uncertainty and change. The Seven Years' War dragged on and petered out, Canada was conquered, America raised the banner of Independence, Warren Hastings organized the trade and government of India; while at home Farmer George reigned feebly and slowly went mad, the Industrial Revolution began in the north, in the south the rick-fires were beacons heralding the Agricultural Revolution, and in the south-west John Wesley's followers kindled fires of a different sort in the hearts of simple men.

Gilbert White's letters contain no mention of these things, no rumour even by which we might tell the pulse of his country-folk in stirring times. Nor is there any anecdote or tittle-tattle of the great men of the day—Washington and Clive, Burke, Wilkes, and Pitt, Dr. Johnson coffee-housing with Boswell at his side. . . . Instead, the letters whisper, oh so softly! of trivial hedgerow happenings, of the blackthorn putting forth its flowers, of the first butterflies sunning on the bank. He has seen a flock of ring-ouzels; he is studying the habits of the mole-cricket; a rare and (he thinks) a new little bird frequents his garden —perhaps it will turn out to be a garden warbler; his tortoise, Timothy, has gone to sleep for the winter; he believes that he has discovered a new species of mouse. Of such trifles are composed the quiet, sweet letters which Gilbert White wrote to his friends and which were afterwards gathered together and published as *The Natural History of Selborne*.

He himself seems to have been as unassuming as his letters, and his life as uneventful. His importance was never any greater than the ordinary, parochial importance of a village parson. He came of a solid, middle-class family; his father was John White, the eldest son of a Fellow of Magdalen, and his mother was the daughter of a rector of

Streatham, Surrey. John White was a barrister of the Middle Temple, but he never had any considerable practice, and he retired from the Bar on his marriage in 1719.

Gilbert was born on the 18th July 1720. We are told that the event occurred 'while the young couple were on a visit to Selborne Vicarage.' Perhaps his parents, when they casually set forth on that 'visit,' did not realize that young Gilbert was so well on his way! At any rate, this is the only evidence we possess of any Bohemian tendencies on the part of this very respectable couple. They settled at Compton in Surrey, where they proceeded to have seven more children; then they moved to East Harting, in Sussex, where they contrived to add one more to a quiver which, in less prodigal times, might well have been thought to be full; and finally they returned to Selborne in 1729 and resided at 'The Wakes,' where they made up the total of their offspring to a round dozen before Mrs. White wearily died.

Of Gilbert's brothers the most noteworthy are: Thomas, a business man, who became an F.R.S. and contributed to the *Gentleman's Magazine*; Benjamin, partner to Whiston, the Fleet Street publisher, who published many of the principal natural history books of the day, including Pennant's *British Zoology* and Gilbert's own *Selborne;* and

John, who was chaplain to the garrison of Gibraltar and who compiled a *Flora Calpensis* which was unfortunately lost after his death. Gilbert corresponded with him regularly, and received from him both specimens and notes.

Gilbert's own career was, as we have said, entirely without eventfulness. He was educated at Basingstoke Grammar School, whence he went up to Oriel College in December 1739. While he was at Oxford he kept an account-book which seems to show that his only extravagance was the indulgence in an attack of smallpox, which cost him no less than £31 10s. This sum includes the fees of two doctors and a nurse, and the cost of such aids to convalescence as wine, green tea, currants, tripe, and rushlights. In spite of this strange fare he made a complete recovery, for within two months he was buying skates and a shooting-net.

Previous to this misfortune, Gilbert had been elected a Fellow of his college and had taken his M.A. degree. He became curate of Swarraton, Hants, at a stipend of £20 a year; but apparently only Sunday duty was expected of him, for he continued to reside at Oxford, making the journey to Swarraton on horseback every week-end. In 1749 he was ordained priest, and thereafter he held a number of temporary posts (including the

Junior Proctorship of Oxford University) and a succession of brief curacies, until he finally settled at Selborne and became the owner—by his uncle's death—of the house called 'The Wakes,' in which he lived for the rest of his days.

His appearance—if we may make a guess from some rather incomplete descriptions—was not particularly striking. He was only five feet three inches tall, and 'slender in person.' He possessed, however, 'a very upright carriage and a presence not without dignity.' We are told also that 'the expression of his countenance was intelligent, kindly, and vivacious.' His portrait was never painted—from which omission it is conjectured that the smallpox permanently disfigured him; but there exists a pen-and-ink sketch of his head, drawn by a friend, T. C., on the fly-leaf of his copy of Pope's *Iliad*, Volume III. (Volume I bears on its fly-leaf this interesting inscription: 'Given me by Mr. Alexander Pope on my taking the degree of B.A., June 30th 1743.') The sketch is not remarkable for any skill of execution, and there is no special reason to conclude that it was necessarily a good likeness. It represents a rather sharp-faced person, with a big nose, very prominent eyes, and a slightly receding forehead. There is a second, unsigned sketch on the fly-leaf of Volume V, which shows a face in profile, and from which one receives the same impression of sharpness and beakiness, and of a rather staring expression in the wide-open eyes.

This, then, or something like this, was the appearance of the little Selborne parson whose letters, so sweetly whispering, have refused to go the dustward way of fading ink and crumbling paper. He was small and short-legged, and perhaps he had a little of the sharp, perky air of those finches and warblers which he so patiently watched. He rode about his parish perched on the back of a preposterous animal which (like the parson's 'lean, sorry jackass of a horse' in *Tristram Shandy*) must have been full brother to Rosinante. On one famous occasion he lent the creature to his friend Mulso, who speedily returned it with the following comment: 'First, he is broken-winded, and wheezes so loud that my heart-ache will do me more harm than good; next, I was forced to carry his head; then, he is intolerably shabby, and will not go at a hand-gallop without constant excitement with whip and spur.'

Upon this sorry-looking beast and others of its kind Gilbert White rode about his beloved countryside and performed, as diligently as any country parson of his time, the duties and visitations of his cure. He seems to have been a tolerant, kindly, easy-going person. Like Herrick, he was fond of children and all young people. He took pleasure in watching the 'frolics' of the latter, and he gave small bounties to the former when they showed him birds' nests or brought him specimens. There is a pleasant line in his *Journal* when he gravely notes the date when the game of hop-scotch was first played on the village green.

We may imagine that his parochial duties were not particularly arduous. On Sundays he must preach, but his sermons were probably stock ones which required little preparation. They contain no mention of natural history, and their style is not the light and airy style of Gilbert White; 'the turgidity of a hundred divines' (as someone has neatly put it) is fearfully apparent in them. One is guilty of an unworthy suspicion that they were purchased in Fleet Street for a shilling or two apiece!

Apart from the wearisome necessity of this hebdomadal homily, to which his stolid country-folk listened with an air of dutiful boredom, Gilbert White had very little work to do in the small parish. There would be an occasional festivity to attend (he notes casually in his *Naturalist's Journal* that one afternoon he sat down to tea with fifty-four young girls, all 'except a few, natives of this place'); then there would often be some poor body who tiresomely required to be baptized, married, or buried; and there would be necessary visits of charity to the Selborne poor. (In an early letter to Thomas Pennant, White remarks with a curious detachment, 'We abound with poor,' but adds comfortably that 'Many of them are sober'.) Finally there would be sick people to be cheered and comforted, and Gilbert White would set off upon that broken-winded creature that was full brother to Rosinante or first cousin to Yorick's horse, to call upon some outlying parishioner who had fallen ill.

This duty done the parson would ride slowly home, making a longer journey of it, perhaps, in order to ride through the Hanger or to look for rare plants in the bogs of Bin's Pond. He would notice the different ways the birds had of flying and perching and walking on the ground. 'When redstarts shake their tails they move them horizontally, *as dogs do when they fawn*; the tail of a wagtail, when in motion, bobs up and down *like that of a jaded horse.*' What sharp eyes he had! But perhaps the simile came quicker to mind because his own Rosinante was so frequently tired, so difficult to push along. . . . Riding on, he sees that 'magpies and jays flutter with powerless wings, and make no despatch.' Watching the swifts carefully, he decided that they pair on the wing. (Nobody had noticed that before.) He remarks that pigeons, unlike most birds, which 'drink sipping at intervals,' 'take a long-continued draught, like quadrupeds.' As he jogs down Wood Lane at evening he sees the goatsucker 'glance in the dusk on the tops of trees like a meteor.'

And with these vivid trifles in his mind he would return at last to his study and his precious books —precious because in his time they were not always easily obtained. He had Ray's *Methodus Plantarum* and Hudson's *Flora Anglica* and Philip Miller's *Gardener's Dictionary*, and a shelf-full of Linnaeus, Geoffroy, Réaumur, Derham, Dr. Hales, Stillingfleet, and Willoughby. Among these books he would sit down and write those grave, quiet, scholarly letters—to Thomas Pennant, Daines Barrington, William Markwick, Robert Marsham; and what letters they were! The Muse alone knows into what magic ink-well he dipped his pen; but I think 'the love of little things' had something to do with it—that same very quiet and yet somehow very eager delight in the sweet trifles of the English countryside which gave a strange wistfulness to the catalogue in Rupert Brooke's poem:

. . . Footprints in the dew;
And oaks; and brown horse-chestnuts, glossy-new;
And new-peeled sticks; and shining pools on grass. . . .

Such loves, I think, were Gilbert White's also. It was 'the pain, the calm, and the astonishment' of a lover that set his unaffected prose so magically glowing. He possessed that tiptoe feeling of wonder and surprise which, I think, all great writers must sometimes feel. Chiffchaffs, though 'no bigger than a man's thumb, fetch an echo out of the Hanger at every note.' The blackcap's song has such 'a wild sweetness' that it always brings to his mind some lines from *As You Like It*. No one has ever described birds, and the songs of birds, as well as Gilbert White. He loved them all, but most he loved the small modest merry-voiced twitterers of the hedgerow and the copse: the wood wren, that little yellow entity that makes 'a sibilous shivering noise in the tops of tall woods'; the grasshopper warbler which, though it may be a hundred yards away, whispers as though it were close by, and which creeps mouse-like through the bottom of the thorns; the flycatcher, with his 'little inward wailing note'; the sedge warbler, 'a delicate polyglot'; and the gold-crested wren, which White delightfully speaks of as 'that shadow of a bird.'

There are five perfect miniatures, five portraits as quick and vivid as Thorburn's. The tiny reedy songs which are so light that they seem to float away on the breezes, the small swelling throats, the fluffed-out feathers, and the busy flutterings, are all caught in a few simple words. You can almost see the leaves on the swaying branch whence the song so surprisingly comes, and the green-gold glow of the sun shining through them.

There is more magic from the ink-well when Gilbert White comes to describe the passage of the seasons and the lovely changeableness of English weather. It is 'a cool sweet day' or 'a delicate warm day,' or the storm comes up in thunder-time in the shape of 'vast, swagging, rock-like clouds' appearing in the distance. August is 'by much the most mute month'; for the birds are silent, and the great winds do not blow. The terrible earthquake summer of 1783 is vividly described. 'The sun, at noon, looked as blank as a clouded moon, and shed a rust-coloured ferruginous light on the ground, and floors of rooms; but was particularly lurid and blood-coloured at rising and setting.' And here, for contrast, is a snowscape of the 'rugged Siberian weather' of 1776. 'Many of the narrow roads were now filled above the tops of the hedges, through which the snow was driven into most romantic and grotesque shapes. . . . Tamed by the season, skylarks settled in the streets of towns, because they saw the ground was bare; rooks frequented dunghills close to houses, and crows watched horses as they passed, and greedily devoured what dropped from them; hares came into men's gardens, and scraping away the snow, devoured such plants as they could find.

'On the 22nd [of January] the author had occasion to go to London, through a sort of Laplandian scene, very wild and grotesque indeed. [In London] the pavements of the streets could not be touched by the horses' feet, so that the carriages ran about without the least noise. Such an exemption from din and clatter was strange, but not pleasant; it seemed to convey an uncomfortable idea of desolation—"*ipsa silentia terrent.*"'

After the snow came the frost. The Thames was frozen over, 'so that crowds ran about on the ice.' The snow now 'crumbled and trod dusty, and, turning grey, resembled bay-salt.' Then suddenly, on the 2nd of February, it begins to thaw, and Gilbert White's sharp eyes notice 'little insects frisking and sporting in a courtyard in South Lambeth, as if they had felt no frost.' He spares a thought for them, wondering 'why the juices in the small bodies and smaller limbs of such minute beings are not frozen.'

No small thing comes amiss to him as a subject for correspondence. For instance, the twenty-third letter to Daines Barrington, which is written in a prose as light as gossamer itself, is concerned solely with a description of those bright filmy cobwebs which seem to fall from the skies when the autumn dews fall. He knew that a host of small spiders made them, but he could not explain 'why these apterous insects should take such a wonderful aerial excursion, and why their webs should at once become so gross and material as to be considerably more weighty than air, and to descend with precipitation.' This greatly puzzled him, and he hazarded a guess which happened to be wrong. Scientific knowledge was not far advanced in his day, and guesses were often wrong; for a naturalist had little data to help him, save that collected by his own observations, and a guess without reliable data is always a shot in the dark. Knowing this, the fact that Gilbert White was sometimes mistaken is not so surprising as the fact that he was so often right. His world was a puzzling world indeed; there was an adventure in every thought. Even such a matter as the copulation of frogs gave rise to wild conjectures; 'the generation of eels' (which had so troubled old Izaak Walton's brain) was still 'dark and mysterious'; and many instructed people still believed that frogs came down to the earth in showers of rain, that the fern-owl sucked milk from the udders of goats, and that cancer could be cured by the application of toads. Poor little shrew mice were walled up alive in holes drilled in ash trees, and the twigs of the trees used as a remedy for ailing horses, cattle, and sheep. And even John Wesley believed in the existence of witchcraft.

Gilbert White scoffed at such superstitions; the practice of drowning, in horse-ponds, 'superannuated wretches, crazed with age,' he considered too gross for his enlightened times. Nor did he believe in the miraculous showers of frogs, the efficacy of the shrew ash, or the good faith of the 'cancer-doctress' who treated that terrible disease by the application of toads. Even he, however, was not infallible; to each man his own private and particular heresy, and Gilbert White's heresy concerned the winter disappearance of swallows. With a most obstinate perversity he cherished the belief that these birds hibernated in England. He had seen laggard swallows and house-martins as late as November, and he had noticed that the disappearing swifts in autumn seemed 'bleached, and, as it were, what country people call piss-burnt, like an old weather-beaten wig.' He devised the fantastic theory that this bleaching was due to the sun's heat, and he reasoned ingenuously that if the swifts followed the sun into lower latitudes they would be still more bleached and woebegone when they returned; whereas he knew that in fact they were as smart and bright in April as if they had just come from moulting. No: they must surely retire to rest and change their feathers; and those late swallows and martins, how could such 'poor little birds' bear up against the rain and snow and equinoctial winds, and the 'meteorous turbulences' of many seas? The conclusion was that they hid themselves in sand quarries or coppice undergrowths or, bat-like, in church towers and cliffs. So Gilbert White peered into the old nests of sand-martins in November, grubbed up bushes on a hill-side, and explored 'the shrubs and cavities' of the south-east end of the Hanger in early spring, in order to discover 'the secret dormitories' of these elusive and puzzling birds. The fact that he found no trace of them did not in the slightest shake his preposterous certainty that they were somewhere to be found; and once he flirted with the wild notion that they retired into the mud at the bottom of ponds. Even a letter from his brother John, who had had 'ocular demonstration' of the seasonal movements of *Hirundines* backwards and forwards across the Straits of Gibraltar, did not seriously disturb his cherished theory, but merely caused him to modify it slightly. Perhaps a portion of the swallow population went abroad; but the remainder undoubtedly hibernated in England!

By this time he was as deeply sunk in his error as the villagers who believed that the earth was flat, in Mr. Kipling's story, and however overwhelming the evidence, I do not think he would have changed his mind. His theory could not be proved, but on the other hand until every bush had been pulled up in the Hanger, until every pond had been drained dry and every old building stripped of its rafters, it could not be conclusively disproved. In fact it was a gloriously unassailable theory, and Gilbert White hung on to it tenaciously until he died. Only two months before his death he set forth with Dr. Chandler, who was presumably another heretic, and tore down the ragged thatch of an empty house in Selborne. Alas, they found no swallows; but three days later White was told by 'a sober hind' that some sand-martins had been seen in the neighbourhood, and although the month was April he decided that they must have emerged from their 'secret *latebrae*' and was 'confirmed' in his suspicions by the news. This made up for his disappointment at finding no swallows in the thatch, and he died with his strange faith intact.

For my part, I am glad that he did not abandon his theory. Somehow his queer perversity makes him seem more human. Even as Homer sometimes nods and Achilles is vulnerable at the heel,

THE HANGER, SELBORNE
(J. A. Symington)

so the great naturalist is not always right; and I think I can see him more clearly now. I can see him tottering along with his friend, on those very short legs of his (for Rosinante bore him no more), and poking his stick into the musty rotten thatch of the old cottage, shaking his head over it, and expecting a swallow to pop out, like the little bird from the camera lens, at every poke. He is a very English figure, this little parson. He has found nothing to support his theory, but never mind, there are plenty of other things in his small world to occupy and interest him. He goes a-simpling and brings back an armful of the sweet plants which have old sweet names—gill-goby-ground, calf's snout, high taper, wild williams, St. Barnaby's thistle, thorough-wax, and clown's allheal. On the recommendation of Dr. Chandler (that hopeful experimentalist!) he makes, and actually drinks, a cup of lime-blossom tea. He plants out mullein and foxglove in his garden. He jots down a recipe for plaster. He investigates the origin of fairy-rings. He counts his cucumbers with delight, and proudly rejoices in his melons. Alas, the frost comes and destroys the melons. He is very upset about it, but he soon forgets them and finds other interests. He makes the discovery that worms are hermaphrodite. He studies the crickets of his own hearth and notes whimsically that 'a good

Christmas fire is to them like the heats of the dog-days.' He makes mushroom ketchup and bottles raisin wine. He laughs at Timothy the tortoise, sheltering from the rain. 'Though it has a shell which would secure it against the wheel of a loaded cart, yet does it discover as much solicitude about rain as a lady dressed in all her best attire, shuffling away on the first sprinklings and running its head up in a corner.'

Sometimes he reads Horace with his young nephew, John White, or tries Phaedrus, in vain, with another nephew, Dick, who is not fond of books and proves an inept pupil. So Gilbert White teaches him to ride and hopes piously that a good seat on a horse may be more useful to him than Virgil or Horace. Young people come often to the house, and sometimes there is dancing as late as half-past four.

In his study, when bad weather keeps him at home, Gilbert White tries his hand at the composition of poetry. He is not very good at it, but he has the classic manner:

> The chilling night dews fall:—away, retire;
> For see, the glow-worm lights her amorous fire!
> Thus, ere night's veil had half obscured the sky,
> Th' impatient damsel hung her lamp on high:
> True to the signal, by Love's meteor led,
> Leander hastened to his Hero's bed.

Occasionally the classic manner leads him dreadfully astray:

These, NATURE'S works, the curious mind employ,
Inspire a soothing melancholy joy;
As fancy warms, a pleasing kind of pain
Steals o'er the cheek, and thrills the creeping vein!

Never mind; just to show that he is not always pompous he will inscribe a Winter Piece to those 'blithe maidens,' the Misses Batty, who frequently visit him; and here it is, so neatly done:

Is this the scene that late with rapture rang,
Where Delphy danced, and gentle Anna sang;
With fairy-step where Harriet tripped so late,
And on her stump reclined the musing Kitty sate?
  Return, dear Nymphs; prevent the purple spring,
Ere the soft nightingale essays to sing;
Ere the first swallow sweeps the freshening plain,
Ere love-sick turtles breathe their amorous pain;
Let festive glee th' enlivened village raise,
Pan's blameless reign, and patriarchal days;
With pastoral dance the smitten swain surprise,
And bring all Arcady before our eyes.

I hope the verses pleased the young ladies, and that they came tripping up to 'The Wakes' to thank him for them; but as likely as not they would find him engaged in some gruesome 'autopsia' upon a dead mouse or bird, which would sorely shock them, and perhaps cause them to swoon.

For such was the parson's thirst for knowledge that although he had 'planted four limes in the butcher's yard, to hide the sight of blood and filth from ye windows,' he would conduct the most hair-raising post-mortems in the interests of science, and on one occasion he made an intrepid examination of the head of a moose-deer belonging to the Duke of Richmond, although the creature was 'in so putrid a state that the stench was hardly supportable.'

But that was more than thirty years ago, in his younger days, and now Parson White is growing old; he would hesitate before undertaking such a long journey as that, all the way to Goodwood to see a dead moose slung up in a stable. Instead, he potters about in his own garden, taking the daily readings of his thermometer, noting the changes of the weather and the passing of the seasons, and watching the flowers come out in their ordered procession each spring. He has finished that perfect miniature, his picture of Selborne village, he has put in every trembling leaf and every twittering bird-song, and now the sight of those sharp eyes is beginning to fade. He administers a gentle reproof to Marsham. 'Pray, good Sir, procure better ink; yours is so pale that it often renders your neat hand scarcely legible!' He is troubled by what he calls 'The Daemon of Procrastination,' so that often letters go long unanswered and specimens long unpacked. Sometimes the dead mice or moles in his study become creeping disasters. . . . But he can still watch the changing skies through his study window, and listen to the gay birds singing from the bushes round his lawn.

'Thus his days passed,' wrote his nephew John (that young John White who had read the Odes of Horace with him as a boy), 'tranquil and serene, with scarcely any other vicissitudes than those of the seasons, till they closed at a mature age on June 26, 1793.' It is a good epitaph; for he had so loved the sweet English seasons that they had become part of his life, and had marked the course of it.

Chapter 7 *The Hunting Men*

THE Muse (as we have seen) has always smiled on anglers; but she has been less kind to the followers of what Izaak Walton called that 'turbulent, toilsome, perplexing recreation,' the chase. Perhaps the delightfully perverse and unreasonable sport of the fishermen brings them close to the Mysteries; perhaps, while seeking the sources of their bright streams, they find, in some magical way, the holy and secret sources of poetry also, so that when they tell of rivers and water-meadows they speak with the tongues of angels. Perhaps there is some similarity about the making of a cast and the making of a sentence; both must be accurate, graceful, rhythmical, and neat. Whatever the reason, it is almost impossible to write very badly about angling; and yet about hunting it seems to be almost equally difficult to write very well. The hands whose hold on the reins is most light and gentle are generally the heaviest and the most inept when it comes to holding a pen.

This is a little strange, for the Muse loves such things as swift movement, bright colour, danger, and a wild cry. She delights in action—or Homer would never have written the *Odyssey* nor Virgil the *Aeneid.* And is not the scarlet of a hunting-coat, vivid against the golden-brown of an autumn coppice, the very colour of which poetry should be made? Yet the Muse is shy of it, and small blame to her; for she has been invoked too often by beefy foxhunters who have tried to suit their metres to the jog-trot of their horses' hoofs, by loud-voiced horse-copers and ungentle squires, and by hearty 'hunting parsons,' the grossness of whose literary style can only be explained by their astonishing unfamiliarity with the Book which it is their profession to teach.

Elusive Muse! Upon no such mortals as these will she bestow her immortal favours. She has had Homer and Milton and Shakespeare for lovers, she has blessed Dante and Heine with her sweet kisses, she has sported with Rabelais, soared above the clouds with Shelley, and danced through the glades of Arcady with Keats. So Whyte-Melville and Adam Lindsay Gordon and the rest of the jog-trot crew must get along as best they can without her aid. It must be confessed that after their own fashion they get along very well. It goes with a swing, but it isn't poetry; *c'est magnifique, mais ce n'est pas la guerre!*

Yet if you were to make an anthology of the literature of the hunting-field, you would have perforce to fill it with much of this brave mediocrity. You could hardly leave out Adam Lindsay Gordon, who wrote verses in the same way as he rode his races—full gallop all the way; and Whyte-Melville would have to go in as well, because he was a gallant gentleman whose gallantry carried him gaily through the difficulties of versification just as it carried him over the tall Leicestershire fences after the Pytchley Hounds. Then you would have to include Somerville—that, to me, most excruciating poet—because he was the greatest authority of his time. 'Nimrod,' famed as a chronicler, would fill a good many undistinguished pages; and the loathly vulgarity of Surtees would fill many more. There would also be a number of joggity-jog poetasters bearing such strange names as Egerton Warburton and Bromley Davenport. *Punch* and the sporting papers would probably provide you with some more.

Three names, however, would stand out in the midst of that dreadful mediocrity and—if your anthology were well-contrived—would relieve the awful sameness of its pages so that the wearied reader, suddenly lighting upon this or that, would cry out in delight: 'Here, here is the Muse's imprint! Here has she breathed a kiss; here she has left her blessing; here, at last, is the authentic whisper of her fluttering wing!' These three oases would be provided respectively by the fine scholarship of Peter Beckford, by the quiet, sweet *Englishness* of Mr. Siegfried Sassoon, and by the poetic skill of Mr. John Masefield, who has made an epic out of a fox-chase for the first time. Let us hasten over the intervening desert as swiftly as we may and visit each oasis in turn.

When Peter Beckford wrote his *Thoughts upon Hare and Foxhunting* in 1779 there were very few books about hunting as we now know it. Gervase Markham's Elizabethan sport was of a more haphazard and less organized kind; and in any case his writings were not easily available. George Turberville had written a little in 1575; and George Gascoigne, in a pleasant poem, had described the somewhat bibulous life of a Lord's Huntsman:

I am the Hunte, which rathe and early rise,
(My bottell filde, with wine in any wise,)
Twoo draughts I drinke, to stay my steps withall,
For eche foot one, bicause I would not falle.
Then take my Hounde, in liam me behinde,
The stately Harte, in fryth or fell to finde.
And whiles I seek his slotte where he hath fedde,
The sweete byrdes sing, to clear my drowsie hedde. . . .

Then I returne, to make a grave reporte,
Whereas I finde, th' assembly doth resorte.
And lowe I crouche, before the Lordlings all,
Out of my Horne, the fewmets lette I fall,
And other signes, and tokens do I tell,
To make them hope, the Harte may like them well.
Then they commaunde, that I the wine should taste,
So biddes mine Arte: and so my throat I baste.

There were also, of course, many descriptions of hunting in the major Elizabethans—Shakespeare, infallible as ever upon any matter within his own experience, was never mistaken in the slightest detail concerning horses and hounds. Finally, there were a few ballads of the chase:

The hunt is up, the hunt is up,
And it is well-nigh day;
And Harry our King is gone hunting,
To bring his deer to bay.

Indeed, any song intended to arouse in the morning—even a love-song—was originally called a *Hunt's-up,* as the French morning-songs were called *aubades*: although admittedly it sounds a little unfitting that a lover should waken his lady in such a fashion.

All these were trifles, however; and Peter Beckford had good reason to complain that in a country 'whose authors sometimes hunt, and whose sportsmen sometimes write' only the practical part of hunting was known. He made an exception in favour of William Somerville, whose poems were published in 1742 and whom he considered to be the only one who had written intelligibly on the subject. This is my sole quarrel with Peter Beckford—that he quotes Somerville on every possible occasion, and professes a deep admiration for him; and although he is probably right when he says that 'the sentiments of Mr. Somerville always do him honour,' I do not think the same can be said of the gentleman's poetry. Here is Mr. Somerville on the choosing of hounds:

> A mean
> Observe, nor the large kind prefer, of size
> Gigantic; he in the thick-woven covert
> Painfully tugs, or in the thorny brake
> Torn and embarrass'd, bleeds. . . .

The *sentiments*, doubtless, are admirable. . . . But better still is the glorious passage in which Somerville gives instructions regarding the proper treatment of bitches upon whom Nature is working her seasonal mischief:

> Mark well the wanton females of thy pack,
> That curl their taper tails, and frisking court
> Their pyebald mates enamour'd: their red eyes
> Flash fires impure; nor rest nor food they take,
> Goaded by furious love. In sep'rate cells
> Confine them now, lest bloody civil wars
> Annoy thy peaceful state.

It is curious that Beckford should have found any merit in this pompous and pretentious stuff; for he himself was the most precise and fastidious of writers. He combined the 'knowledgeableness' of a Master of Foxhounds with the learning of a Westminster scholar; and it has been said of him that 'he would bag a fox in Greek, find a hare in Latin, inspect his kennels in Italian, and direct the economy of his tables in excellent French.' But also he wrote the most admirable English prose, of the sort which has for me the flavour of nuts and old port, taken in the library after dinner, around a sweet wood fire.

Thoughts upon Hunting pretends to be no more than a technical treatise, and as such it may still be read with profit to-day. It gives instructions to a Master of Foxhounds upon such matters as the selection of his pack, the management of his kennel and his stable, the duties of his servants, and the proper manner in which he shall conduct his sport. It might have been the dreariest stuff, and yet there is hardly a page of it that does not give pleasure—for which blessing, I suppose, we must ultimately give thanks to that school which has always taught her sons to read good Latin verse in order that they may write good English prose.

But the Classics, while helping to mould Peter Beckford's style, did more for him than that: they gave him a sense of proportion. He was that *rara avis,* a foxhunter who understood that fox-hunting was not the whole of living. Therefore he made his book a brief one ('Since a great book has long been looked upon as a great evil, I shall take care not to sin that way at least') and he even apologized, very gracefully, for its subject. 'Fox-hunting, however lively and animating it may be in the field, is but a dull, dry subject to write upon; and I can now assure you from experience, that it is much less difficult to follow a fox-chase than to describe one.' How much we should have been spared if the great army of red-faced and red-coated poetasters had realized this!

It is Peter Beckford's great virtue that he knows, and insists continually, that his sport is only 'a trifle' after all. He reads his *Spectator* and he has seen depicted there, 'with infinite humour,' the character of one Will Wimble, who passed his whole life in the pursuit of trifles. '*Touché!*' cries Beckford with the utmost good humour—and proceeds to demonstrate that he is not incapable of laughing at himself. 'It is said, *there is a pleasure in being mad, which only madmen know.*' Thus, half-mockingly, he defends the queer, illogical pursuit in which he finds such delight. 'Triflers there are of every denomination. Are we not all triflers? and are we not told that all is vanity?' Yet 'it must be confessed,' he adds, growing suddenly serious, 'that the man who spends his whole life in trifles, passes it contemptibly, compared with those who are employed in researches after knowledge, or in professions useful to the state.'

Again and again, throughout his book, one hears his dry, faintly mocking laughter—the laughter of a man who is a cynic in the old, full sense of the word; not one of your disgruntled moderns whose thin cackle merely expresses his distaste for the world, but one who has discovered that all things are laughable, including himself. Thus he can afford to smile at the thought of Henry IV of France, who made hunting his chief amusement, so that 'his very love-letters, strange as it may appear,' were filled with little else; and he can tell a wry story against two kings who were triflers too:

'Louis the Fifteenth was so passionately fond of this diversion [hunting] that it occupied him entirely. The King of Prussia [Frederick the Great], who never hunts, gives up a good deal of his time to music, and himself plays the flute. A German, last war, meeting a Frenchman, asked him very impertinently: "*Si son maître chassoit toujours?*" "*Oui, oui,*" replied the other, "*il ne joue jamais de la flute.*"'

Beckford's book is chiefly delightful because, although its subject is one which offers peculiar attractions to monomaniacs, it never forgets that there are other, and more important, things in life. Its author makes the best of both worlds, that of the mind and that of the senses, enlivening a grave discussion on 'scent' with a quotation from Cicero, directing his huntsman how to cast with the aid of a geometrical example, calling upon Martial to witness to the virtues of the hare, *Inter quadrupedes gloria prima lepus*, and reminding the reader that those warm sunless days which are ideal for hunting are called *jours des dames* by the French! And all this, mark you, in the midst of the most minute instructions upon the correct dimensions of kennels and the intricate business of hunting a pack of hounds.

I believe that, for the most part, these instructions still hold good to-day; so that the book has the same dateless practicality as *The Compleat Angler* has. I should not dare to compare it with Walton's book in any other sense; old Izaak's artlessness was better art, I think, than Beckford's studied periods, and I prefer the Elizabethan sunrise to the rather bored heyday of the elegant Georgians. Yet perhaps, if we do not smell the flowers in Beckford's treatise, nor have the feeling that the dryads and the wood-nymphs are very near at hand, the defect is due more to the subject than to the writing itself; for the rank smell of a freshly killed fox is apt to be stronger than the scent of the flowers, and huntsmen are noisier than anglers—their blustering is likely to frighten the dryads and the wood-nymphs away.

Supposing that your anthology is arranged in chronological order, Beckford will be closely followed by C. J. Apperley, who wrote under the pseudonym of 'Nimrod'; and sandwiched between these two we shall find *John Peel,* which was written by John Woodcock Graves about 1825. How shall we define a folk-song? Is it not a song which is known to all, which is very close to the hearts of the people, and which has stood the test of time? Then *John Peel* is a folk-song, just as *Daisy* is; although admittedly *John Peel* has lost some of its 'folk' character by being played as a gallop and sung by semi-intoxicated persons at the ends of hunt-balls—on which occasions, for some extraordinary reason, it is almost always sung incorrectly, 'coat so gay' (with the idea of hunting-pink) being substituted for 'coat so grey' (which was the colour John Peel actually wore).

And now we come to Nimrod, whose *Hunting Tours* has always seemed to me an extremely dull book; but perhaps that is because I have never

JOHN MYTTON

been able to feel very interested in the minutiae of the hunting-field, the histories of past seasons and the characters of notables long dead. On the other hand, Nimrod's *Memoirs of the Life of John Mytton* shared first place with *Struwwelpeter* as one of my childhood's favourites. My copy of it has disappeared in the same inexplicable way as teddy-bears and tin soldiers disappear when one out-grows them. They are not, as far as one knows, given away, and they are not, one piously hopes, consigned to the dustbin or the fire—they just vanish, so that one is tempted to believe that they had some magical quality about them, that they have been called back into the fairy godmother's secret store whence they so magically came. Strangely enough, I have never since seen an edition of the *Memoirs of the Life of John Mytton* which even remotely resembled mine. As far as I can remember it was a fairly large book, and it contained a number of very remarkable illustrations which depicted the still more remarkable incidents of poor John Mytton's life. For instance, there were pictures of the 'Upsetting of the Gig,' of the 'Jumping of the Turnpike,' and of the 'Burning of the Nightshirt,' and there was also—or do I imagine it?—a portrait of John Mytton, barefooted and clad only in a thin shirt, setting out across the ice on a bitter December night to shoot some wild geese which were coming inland with the blizzard.

The stories told beneath these pictures were enough to warm the heart of any boy. The 'Burning of the Nightshirt,' for instance, occurred when Mytton had fled to France to escape his creditors. Retiring to bed at his lodgings, somewhat the worse for drink, he was troubled by a most obstinate hiccup, which all the standard remedies for that complaint proved powerless to cure. 'By God!' said John Mytton, 'I 'll see if I can *frighten it away*'; whereupon he picked up a candle and held it to his nightshirt, which instantly burst into flames. Two of his friends rushed into the room and found him blazing furiously upon the floor; and at last they succeeded in tearing off his nightshirt and putting out the fire. Terribly burned, John Mytton picked himself up and staggered into bed. 'I 've frightened away that damned hiccup,' was all he said. Next morning, although he must have been in agony, he managed to greet his friends with a mighty 'View Halloa.'

The gig story must be told in Nimrod's own words:

'As he was one day driving one of his friends in a gig, who expressed a strong regard for his neck, with a hint that he considered it in some danger, Mytton addressed him thus: "Was you ever much hurt, then, by being upset in a gig?" "No, thank God," said his companion, "for I never was upset in one." "What!" replied Mytton, "never upset in a gig? What a d——d slow fellow you must have been all your life"; and running his near wheel up the bank, over they both went.'

I remember very well the expression of sheer terror on the face of Mytton's friend, in that glorious picture which had been examined so often that it had come away from its bindings and was loose in the book; and there was a wretched horse-dealer, in another picture, who was likewise cursing his fate that he had ever met such a mad March-hare as the young Shropshire squire. This unfortunate person was a man named Clarke, to whom Mytton had given an order to purchase some carriage-horses for him.

'Putting one of them into a gig, tandem, to see, as he expressed it himself, "whether he would make a good leader," he asked the dealer, who sat beside him, if he thought he was a good timber-jumper? On the dealer expressing a doubt, Mytton exclaimed: "Then we'll try him!" and a closed turnpike gate being before him, he gave the horse his head, and a flanker with his whip at the same moment, when he cleared the gate in beautiful style, leaving Mytton and the dealer, and the other horse, all on the nether side of the gate; and fortunately all alive.'

This poor drunken lunatic became one of my heroes; a dangerous hero for a boy who had the love of horses born in him! And perhaps it was owing to John Mytton's baneful influence that I subsequently spent so many Christmas holidays tied up with slings and bandages. There came to the little stable at the bottom of our garden a succession of the wildest, raciest, maddest horses that ever made nuisances of themselves at Boxing Day meets. First there was the bay mare Cinders, who finally capped an eventful three weeks by backing me into a plate-glass shop-window one Sunday afternoon. She was followed by the loveliest black called Judy, a temperamental, highly-strung creature, who would go dancing over the tarmac whenever she saw a motor bus and who smashed up the blacksmith's shop whenever I took her to be shod. And the third of that unholy trinity was a saturnine old racehorse called Brampton, of whom my most vivid memory is that he once ran away with me for the extraordinary distance of six miles, stopping only when he burst a blood-vessel in his nose.

Upon such creatures as these I would frequently ride away for week-ends, staying with friends fifteen or twenty miles away, and carrying my pyjamas and sponge-bag in a haversack; and sometimes I would return as late as twelve o'clock on a Sunday night, to find the family sitting up and anxiously awaiting my homecoming lest I should arrive upon a stretcher. Partly by good luck, and partly because I knew how to fall, I never injured myself very badly; and as for minor dislocations, I was always very proud of them. An arm in a sling was to be regarded as a soldier regards a wound-stripe; and for this curious attitude I believe Nimrod and John Mytton were jointly responsible. It certainly wasn't their fault that I did not break my neck!

Poor John Mytton! The pictures in Nimrod's book did not tell me the other side of his desperate, mad, unhappy career: how he inherited a fortune and wildly spent it, how the eight bottles of port a day soon gave place to nearly as many of brandy, how his friends left him when the money was gone, and how their place was taken by a horde of creditors who first fawned and then bullied, until Jack Mytton fled from them to France. Nor did it tell me of his return to the empty house at Halston, near Shrewsbury, which, in his queer way, he so greatly loved that he could not keep away from it; nor of his inevitable arrest and horrible end amid the dirt and degradation of a debtors' prison, when the eight bottles of brandy were available no more. . . . Wild and wanton I know he was, yet—perhaps because he was my hero when I was a boy—I cannot bear to contemplate the miseries of his end: his screams for the drink which he now so desperately needed, the mockery of the other prisoners, the filth and the awful squalor, the pain and the final madness when the mists of delirium tremens gathered terribly around him, and he was alone against all these horrors, alone and friendless, who had had so many friends. . . .

His wife, whom he loved, had been forced to leave him; and so he was quite without comfort when he died, at the age of thirty-eight, 'worn out by too much foolishness, too much wretchedness, and too much brandy.' The words are Miss Edith Sitwell's, who, in her fascinating book on *The English Eccentrics,* has drawn a picture of him which is more vivid than Nimrod's, and which is kind and wise and pitying as well. She shows him as living always in a furious wind (and indeed great winds seem to have been connected with most of his exploits—it was such a wind that blew a thousand bank-notes out of his carriage on the way back from the races and scattered them like the remnants of a paper-chase all the way down the road, and it was a terrible cruel wind that blew through his thin nightshirt in that picture of his goose-shooting expedition, in Nimrod's book). 'Here he comes,' writes Miss Sitwell. 'Here he comes, that poor driven drunken ghost, blown by a turbulent hurricane weather. His life seemed to be spent in running like an ostrich—he walked as fast and as strongly as that bird—racing, jumping, driving, hunting, chased always by a high mad black wind. He meant, always, to cheat that wind. Let it blow through him and eat him to the bone. He would show it how little he cared.'

That is a better portrait of this 'half-mad hunting hunted creature' than the admiring Nimrod could paint; his crazy spirit had much in common with the crazy winds, and I think Miss Sitwell was right in seeing him as driven, driven always before a whirling, whistling, inescapable gale. . . . A brave, mad, lovable poor devil he was, and I hope he found peace at last, in some place where the great winds blow not. For his epitaph I must quote Miss Sitwell's final words, which have a strange tenderness, and to which I cry 'Amen!'

'I hope that this pitiful creature has found a warm country heaven of horses and hounds, an old and kindly heaven of country habits and country sweetness, with heavenly mansions where he and Baronet can sit by the fire together once more, horse and man, and where the master can forget the dirt and wretchedness of the debtors' prison, and the eight bottles of port a day, and all the ancient foolishness.'

R. S. Surtees was a contemporary of Nimrod, and I do not think it is an exaggeration to say that his *Handley Cross* was at one time the Bible of a certain class of Englishman. Whether it was ever very popular outside that class I am somewhat inclined to doubt. *Ask Mamma, Plain or Ringlets,* and *Mr. Sponge's Sporting Tour* were other volumes from which the Victorian hunting man would quote, and misquote, with gleeful chuckles at every possible opportunity. These books are probably unique in having won the great majority of their readers from the ranks of the Completely Unlettered; many of those who could glibly quote 'Mr. Jorrocks' had never willingly read anything else in their lives. *Handley Cross* was even a sort of Culture; it was creditable that you should know your Jorrocks well. If you were asked: 'What sort of night it was?' and you could reply swiftly: 'Hellish dark and stinks of cheese,' you were certain to provoke roars of laughter—in fact you had laid the foundations of a social success; because your audience would readily remember how the odious Pigg, being asked 'What of the night?' by Mr. Jorrocks, and being in his usual condition of drunken stupidity, had staggered to the cupboard, opened the door, and made that memorable reply.

For my part I must confess that I have never found Surtees very funny; perhaps he was quoted at me too much in my youth. His gallery of genial rascals, crooks, and cadgers seems to me to be singularly unattractive. These rogues are gross without greatness; they are like the characters in *Pickwick Papers* would be if Dickens were stripped of his all-pervading humanity. Moreover, they have none of the vitality with which Dickens animated his people; the only distinctive thing they possess is a certain pungency of speech. Mr. Soapy Sponge, Mr. Facey Romford, Mr. Jorrocks, and James Pigg: what a hideous scare-crow crew they are! A dismal sort of drunkenness, and a petty sort of dalliance with housekeepers and the like, compose their mean pleasures, and for the rest they cadge, cheat, lie, and swindle in a wholly vulgar and unimaginative way. Their antics are no more humorous than those of the horrible people in Rowlandson's cartoons, of which —far more than of John Leach's excellent drawings —they always somehow remind me.

Stripped of its picturesqueness, of its indefinable morning-in-the-country' feeling, and of a certain air of brave pageantry which, whatever its humanitarian opponents may say, it nevertheless possesses, foxhunting would be a dismal and sordid business indeed; and I think it is this very lack of picturesqueness which makes Surtees's descriptions so unpleasing and so dull. If there is no poetry about the business—if there 's no more in it than the chivvying to death of a wretched frightened creature with the aid of twenty couples of hounds—then foxhunting is surely no more than the joyless barbarity which its detractors allege it to be. It is pleasant, therefore, to turn from the contemplation of the rubicund Mr. Jorrocks, holding up the mangled remains of the 'old customer' by the brush, to some more gallant and less bloody spectacle. Even G. J. Whyte-Melville is a relief after Surtees: Whyte-Melville with his insistence that foxhunting is a 'clean' and chivalrous pastime, and one designed by heaven for the benefit of Englishmen of gentle birth. *Katerfelto,* and such jolly verses as *Brow, Bay, and Tray,* are the sort of things which may be read with a good deal of pleasure by boys of sixteen; at least I can well remember the delight which *Katerfelto* gave to me, though I should not care to risk disillusionment by trying to read it to-day. I dare say it would seem very treacly now; for of course Whyte-Melville romanticized foxhunting just as Surtees, in the opposite way, stripped it of any romance which it was capable of possessing. A modern writer, W. H. Ogilvie, has expressed the 'romantic' attitude in some lines addressed to Whyte-Melville himself:

> How good it is, how good, to fling aside
> The last new garbage-novel of the day
> And turn again with pleasure and with pride
> To your long line of volumes silver gray,
> And with you, gallant heart, to ride away
> Through that clean world where your Sir Galahads ride!

Which all sounds very delightful until you remember what a fox looks like when the hounds have had their way with him—and then that clean world suddenly vanishes, the gay Sir Galahads seem to be rather tarnished knights, and you wonder whether the 'last new garbage-novel' (which is probably one of Aldous Huxley's or Richard Aldington's) is not after all a more useful contribution to the cause of humanity than that torn and bleeding fox, and the senseless 'whoo-hooping.'

Both Surtees and Whyte-Melville, I think, lacked imagination. Surtees failed to hear the music which is older and deeper than that of the horn and the holloaing—the beat of the horse-hoofs and the lovely and terrifying cry of the hounds; and Whyte-Melville, dazzled by the gay pageantry of it all, could not spare a thought for the throbbing pulses and the bursting heart of the little red fox which toiled so painfully towards the stopped earth.

Neither of these writers ever came near to greatness; and I wonder whether the reason is not to be found partly in their lack of pity—which is a very different thing from sentimentality. Surtees had no pity for his people, and Whyte-Melville had no pity for his fox. It is interesting to compare them with two modern writers who have written of foxhunting with understanding and yet with that wide and comprehensive compassion which includes both hunter and hunted, man and beast.

Mr. Siegfried Sassoon's *Memoirs of a Foxhunting Man* is the sort of book which Surtees might have written if he had been able to make us smell the green English pastures and the brown English woodlands—if he had known that these loved things were as much a part of foxhunting as the blood and the shouting. Yet its manner is as quiet as Surtees's was noisy; it is a book without high-lights and without a climax, so that its effect is almost that of the hack home in the dark after a long day. It is a wistful looking-back on something which has gone for ever—the England that was before the War; and its cool, simple, delightful prose is the perfect vehicle for such 'recollecting in tranquillity.' Such a quiet sweetness it has, such a tenderness, such an 'aesthetic awareness' (to use a phrase of Sir John Squire's), that it leaps right out of that imaginary anthology and takes its place, not in the limited literature of foxhunting, but in the literature of the English language, in company with Walton's *Compleat Angler* and White's *Selborne* and Cobbett's *Rural Rides,* and the works of Hudson and Edward Thomas and all the others who have loved 'the sweet three corners' of England.

Mr. John Masefield is the other modern writer who has found in foxhunting a subject fit for his fancy. But while Mr. Sassoon, deliberately choosing the most austere prose for his medium, has painted in soft colours a scene from which the light is fading, Mr. Masefield has given us a glorious galloping poem, as colourful and vivid as a picture by Lionel Edwards, as full of sunlight as a canvas by Munnings. Indeed, I know few scenes in literature which are more happily flooded with the sunlight of an English morning than the Meet in *Reynard the Fox,* when the country people ride up one by one and two by two on to the broad green strip of sward outside 'The Cock and Pye.' This first part of the poem serves as a prologue to the story of the great run; and I had almost written that word 'prologue' with a capital

'P,' for the thing is very Chaucerian in its swift sharp characterization, in its vigorous, earthy, colloquial style, and in its intense *Englishness*. Meeting Mr. Masefield's Parson as he rides up to the inn ('The parson was a manly one'), you feel that you are meeting again the monk in the *Canterbury Tales*:

An out-rydere, that loved venerye;
A manly man, to been an abbot able.
Ful many a deyntee hors hadde he in stable;
And, when he rood, men mighte his brydal here
Ginglen in a whistling wind as clere,
And eke as loude as dooth the chapel-belle.

And is not Mr. Masefield's Doctor ('A smiling silent man whose brain Knew all of every secret pain') a reincarnation of Chaucer's 'verrey parfit practisour' who

Knew the cause of everich maladye,
Were it of hoot or cold, or moiste, or drye?

So they ride up one by one and two by two, these changeless undying ones who are not so much English characters as pieces of England herself: the old ploughman with his 'gaunt, burnt face,' the squire, 'an old bear in a scarlet pelt'; Richard, the doctor's son:

As merry as a yearling is
In May-time in a clover patch;

Bill Ridden with his hard, horse-coper's mouth, and his lovely daughter Belle, who was so shy that

> The kittens in the barley-mow,
> The setter's toothless puppies sprawling,
> The blackbird in the apple calling,
> All knew her spirit more than we,
> So delicate these maidens be
> In loving lovely helpless things.

Then there are Nob and Cob and Bunny Manor, wild young fellows who know the joys of drinking with the stable-lads and singing coarse songs and 'damning people's eyes and guts Or drawing evening-church for sluts'; there is the soldier home from the Afghan frontier, 'Lean, puckered, yellowed, knotted, scarred, Tough as a hide-rope twisted hard'; there is the old farmer from the Vale who is 'much like a robin in the face' and who possesses 'the russet-apple mind That betters as the weather worsen'; there is the Condicote clergyman, a very Chaucerian figure indeed:

> A pommle cob came trotting up,
> Round-bellied like a drinking-cup,
> Bearing on back a pommle man,
> Round-bellied like a drinking-can;

and there is Tom Dansey the first whip:

> He loved the English countryside;
> The wine-leaved bracken in the ride,
> The lichen on the apple trees,
> The poultry ranging on the lees,

The farms, the moist, earth-smelling cover,
His wife's green grave at Mitcheldover,
Where snowdrops pushed at the first thaw.
Under his hide his heart was raw
With love and pity of these things.

But the loveliest portrait of all is that of young Cothill on his chestnut mare, young Cothill who 'loved the downland like a sea':

So beautiful he was, so bright,
He looked to men like young delight
Gone courting April maidenhood
That has the primrose in her blood,
He on his mincing lady mare.

At last the hounds move off, a bright pool around the huntsman, 'Their colour like the English weather, Magpie and hare, and badger-pye,' and the cavalcade trots off behind them, a cavalcade that is as old as England and as much a part of her as the young wheat pricking the brown ploughlands and the tall wine-coloured elms and the red and white roses coming out on the larch.

They are very real, these characters of Mr. Masefield's—as real and English and alive as Chaucer's pilgrims who rode down the green way to Canterbury on just such a bright morning as this more than five hundred years ago. One has only to meet them to realize why Surtees and Whyte-Melville failed. Neither Surtees's cheapjack Cockneys nor Whyte-Melville's chivalrous Sir Galahads ever came out of the English soil like the young springing wheat; they were never very close to the heart of England, nor had they ever any real connection with foxhunting, which has long been an integral part of the life of the countryside. Whyte-Melville's heroes were chivalrous abstractions; Surtees's people were puppets endowed with a rather racy manner of speech. Neither ever existed among the grey villages and the short-cropped downlands and the brown dripping woods, and all the sweetness and roughness and tenderness and bitterness which is English weather and English country life.

The second part of Mr. Masefield's poem tells the epic story of the Ghost Heath Run; and it is Reynard the Fox who is the chief character in the drama now. There is an exquisite description of his wanderings and mating on the previous night, and of his first awareness of danger when he heard the hounds coming to Ghost Heath Wood:

> He moved to his right to a clearer space,
> And all his soul came into his face,
> Into his eyes and into his nose,
> As over the hill a murmur rose.

Indeed it is chiefly through his flexed ears and sharp eyes and wise nose that we experience the incidents of the hunt—the doubtful fluty whimperings when the pack checks, the full crashing terrifying cry as they race over the meadows where the scent hangs heavy, the thin far note of the horn, and the shouting of men, which of all sounds is the most horrible to a hunted creature. We feel, with him, the gradual coming-on of fear (for Mr. Masefield knows that a fox's fear only begins with his weariness), and as his brush goes down in the mud we detect a new note in the wild high crying behind him: death in it, and a terrible eagerness for blood.

When a terrier courses him, and spoils his scent, we know exactly what the respite feels like to him:

> He felt that the unseen link that bound
> His spine to the nose of the leading hound
> Was snapped, that the hounds no longer knew
> Which way to follow nor what to do.

But soon they are on it again, they are running joyfully with 'spear-straight sterns,' 'the horn's soft laughter' is close behind him with its 'leu, leu, leu' which chills the blood—and as with his limbs stiffening and his brush all muddy and the beating of blood like thunder in his head he makes his last spurt for shelter, he feels the first failure of courage which is the coming of death.

> He thought as he ran of his old delight
> In the wood in the moon in an April night,

His happy hunting, his winter loving,
The smells of things in the midnight roving,
The look of his dainty-nosing, red,
Clean-felled dam with her footpads' tread.
Of his sire, so swift, so game, so cunning,
With craft in his brain and power of running,
Their fights of old when his teeth drew blood.
Now he was sick, with his coat all mud.

The earth which would have given him sanctuary is stopped—filled with stones; and it would be all up with Reynard the Fox were not Mr. Masefield compassionate. He has run him to a standstill, he has run him till the pumping heart will pump no longer, and now the fox lies in the thorns with his teeth bared and his ears flexed back, waiting for the hounds. But Mr. Masefield cannot bring himself to kill him. A fresh fox gets up before the pack and on they go; and since hounds must kill or a hunt is not well ended, they pull down this fresh fox in the open just before dark, after the fastest and longest run that Dansey can remember. As for Reynard:

The stars grew bright in the winter sky,
The wind came clean with a tang of frost,
The brook was troubled for new things lost,
The copse was happy for old things found,
The fox came home and he went to ground.

I think Mr. Masefield's poem is a great one because it is filled with that aloof and god-like compassion which is a poet's part, and which is never tinged with sentimentality or the propagandist's desire to emphasize pros and cons. It never forgets the wild beauty which lives even in the terrible crying of the hounds—the strange poetry of fear and pain and death. It does not leave out the picturesqueness and the high ecstasy without which hunting would be merely a matter of dirt and blood and the mangling of a beautiful creature. It has all the colour and all the sweet smells of the English countryside in it; and yet it is aware of the cruelty and the lust also, and it has pity for the terror of a hunted thing—pity that almost tears your heart out.

No sensitive person can write about foxhunting or read about it without being aware of this aspect of it. You may love it because it gives you a gallop over the downs, because you are fond of the wet-smelling winter coverts and the brave picture which red coats make, or because the 'Ai, ai, ai' of the hounds in cry stirs something in you which you cannot explain; but unless you are very hard and insensitive you cannot deny that there are certain aspects of it which you dare not think about—you must deliberately shut out of your mind the picture of a beaten fox or you will never ride after the hounds again. At least I know that it is so with me; and while I have been writing this chapter I have become increasingly aware of a note which runs inevitably through the whole literature of foxhunting—a note which sounds like an echo of Macbeth's dreadful cry: 'It will have blood.' Five years ago I do not think I should have heard it at all; but five years ago I was only one-and-twenty. I know that if I heard the hunt come tittupping down the road outside my house this morning I should be out and after them like a rat after the Pied Piper of Hamelin; and yet I am wondering whether, in another five years' time, I shall not prefer to ride over the hills alone, on days when hounds are not hunting, when the lolloping hares of the downland pause and sit up and watch me unafraid, when the white-tipped fox-cubs sit on the top of their earth and listen to the clickety-clack of my tittupping without hearing the other sound which is generally associated with horse-hoofs—the swift padding of the pack, and the lovely and terrible cry of them.

Chapter 8 *Politics and Swedes*

William Cobbett was nearly sixty when he rode across half England, and he must have been as tough as an old English oak, since on one occasion he went up to the top of the South Downs in the wind and the rain in order to cure a persistent cough! He was rather like the traditional figure of John Bull; he had a red face and white hair crowning it, like snow on a berry. It is related by Heine that he had a 'scolding Radical laugh'; certainly he had a most ungentlemanly habit of shouting. His son, young Richard, rode like Echo beside him, dutifully responding 'Yes, father,' 'Indeed, father,' while Cobbett discoursed at the top of his voice upon such matters as the proper cultivation of swedes, the villainy of 'the monster Malthus,' the viciousness of tea-drinking, the worthlessness of potatoes as an article of food, and the crass stupidity, the downright wickedness, of anybody who happened to disagree with his very violent opinions. He sang also (to young Richard and to the brown, wet English lanes) a paeon in praise of the virtues of William Cobbett: his industry, his good sense, his excellent health, his temperate habits, his stout-heartedness in adversity, and his ultimate inevitable triumph over his enemies. 'If accident had not taken me from the plough, many a villain would have slept at peace by day and swaggered about at night.'

'Yes, father . . .' said Richard.

And then, no doubt, Richard became a dutiful listener, for the hundredth time, to the fantastic story of his father's life. What a tale it was!—the saga of the innkeeper's son who ran away from home, enlisted in the army, and became sergeant-major of his regiment in two years; who taught himself grammar and forged for himself a vivid prose-style while copying out the orders of the day; who left the army, involved himself in politics, and stormed and raged with such effect, both in England and America, that the world was compelled to listen to him; who engaged in more furious controversies, published more pamphlets, and edited more newspapers than anybody had ever done before; who was fined for libel, imprisoned for sedition, and made bankrupt—and who not only survived these adversities, but drew fresh vigour from them. . . . Poor Richard's brain must have become quite dizzy as it tried to keep pace with the twistings and turnings of that incredible story; because the story did not march in a straight line, as do those of more orderly lives—it digressed and wandered and digressed again, and became connected, in some extraordinary fashion, with tea and potatoes and acacia trees, and 'Cobbett's Corn' and the bones of Tom Paine, and swedes, swedes, always swedes!

It would require a book as long as Mr. G. D. H. Cole's excellent biography [1] to tell with sober gravity and a sense of proportion the extraordinary story of Cobbett's life. Sketched briefly here, it will sound more giddy, more extravagant, and more improbable than the wildest of Hollywood's scenarios; it will frequently sound comic, and sometimes ridiculous; and it will inevitably produce the impression of something between a melodrama and a farce.

It begins on the 9th of March in the year 1763, when Cobbett was born (very fittingly) at an inn called the 'Jolly Farmer,' at Farnham in Surrey, of good peasant stock. His father, starting life as a labourer, had saved enough money to become

[1] *The Life of William Cobbett*, by G. D. H. Cole. Collins, 1924.

a small farmer and an innkeeper as well, and had also acquired a smattering of education, which he passed on to his son. William picked up what he could of reading, writing, and arithmetic in the evenings, and spent his days scaring the rooks from the turnip seed and the hungry pigeons from the corn. Later he was promoted to the more responsible tasks of hoeing and ploughing and driving the team at harvest-time.

At the age of eleven, for no particular reason, he ran away from home and took service in the gardens at Kew. On his way thither he spent his last threepence in buying a copy of Swift's *Tale of a Tub*: a sufficiently eccentric beginning for a very eccentric career. When he tired of Kew he returned to Farnham and the life of a farmer's boy. He loved 'fairs, cricket matches, and hare-hunts,' and the labours of the field; but he could not forget now that there was a world elsewhere. When he was nineteen he made another attempt to escape into this wider world; he went to Portsmouth and tried to join the navy. Unfortunately the captain of the *Pegasus* man-o'-war misunderstood his motives. In *his* experience of recruiting it was not often the spirit of adventure which moved stolid farmers' lads to run away to sea; more probably there had been some moon-mad June-night philandering in the hayfield, and now a lass was begging to be taken to the altar before the child came. 'It is better to be led to church in a halter,' said the bluff sea-captain, 'than to be tied to a gangway or married to *Miss Roper*.' Young Cobbett blushed in his innocence, thereby increasing the captain's suspicions, and was promptly sent ashore. He returned to the plough, but he was 'spoiled for a farmer,' and next spring he ran away again, this time to London. Here he worked for nine dark and miserable months as a lawyer's clerk, slaving by candle-light from five in the morning until eight or nine at night, in a sort of dungeon which formed part of Gray's Inn; he was provided for by an ancient hag with whom it would wrong the Witch of Endor to compare her; and he never quitted this gloomy recess save on Sundays, when he walked in Saint James's Park. During one of these walks he noticed an advertisement inviting all loyal young men, who had a mind to gain riches and glory, to join His Majesty's Marines and 'have the peculiar honour and happiness of being enrolled in the Chatham Division.' Cobbett went down to Chatham next day, took a shilling to drink His Majesty's health, and by some mischance found himself, not a marine, but a private soldier in the 54th Foot.

Next year he went with his regiment to New

Brunswick. He had already been promoted to the rank of corporal and appointed copyist to the commandant of the garrison; and thus, as he laboriously translated into plain English the reports of half-literate company commanders, he learned how to write good prose. Surely a great writer never served his apprenticeship in a stranger school! And perhaps Cobbett's style bears some trace still of the barrack and the orderly-room. It has a military precision and a military pace; it marches, it keeps step, but it also has a tendency to become rather noisy. It is probably the best prose of its sort that has ever been written; but it retains the manner of the N.C.O. There's no quick, clever swordsmanship about it, no elegant officer's stuff; instead it goes off with a bang like that of a musket. Here are no 'antic, lisping, affected fantasticoes' such as Mercutio complained of; in the place of a sword's swift fancy there is a blunderbuss —but the most accurate blunderbuss that has ever been devised.

At the age of twenty-three Cobbett was made sergeant-major of his regiment. (Whatever his walk of life, he would never be content to be anything less than a phenomenon!) In his various autobiographical writings, scattered through the *Political Register, Advice to Young Men,* and *The Life and Adventures of Peter Porcupine,* he tells the story of his military experiences with an egotism which is so unbounded that it delights rather than repels. He was superbly contemptuous of 'his supreme jackasses,' the officers, who were a drunken, roystering, pilfering crew, and whose intellects were so pitifully small that they could not appreciate the difference between a semicolon and a comma! Their ignorance of the rudiments of grammar gave Cobbett a feeling of great superiority over them. He claims to have done most of their work a great deal better than they could have done it themselves; in fact one gets the impression that he ran the whole regiment. As a reward for some specially good achievement he was given leave to go off up country 'to see an old farmer and his family, and to shoot pigeons.' He not only shot pigeons, he also fell in love; and of course, being Cobbett, he must needs fall in love in an entirely original and preposterous way. As he was out walking, early one morning, he saw a young girl scrubbing a wash-tub outside her house. He decided at once that she was beautiful (for that, he had always said, should be an indispensable qualification); but he also saw in her marks of a certain 'sobriety of conduct' which, even more than her beauty, attracted him to her. 'That 's the girl for me,' he said—and made up his mind then and there that she should one day become his wife. At this time she was thirteen, and he twenty-one.

He subsequently described the manner of his falling in love in his *Advice to Young Men*; and he finished the paragraph telling of his love-at-first-sight with a piece of the most delicious egotism. 'So that this matter was at once settled as firmly as if written in the book of fate.' Thus determinedly did William Cobbett woo! And although the Fates did their best to rob him of his chosen bride (for his regiment was moved and, being away from her for two years, he very nearly fell in love with someone else!), Cobbett got the better of them in the end. Ann, his first choice, went to England with the artillery regiment in which her father was a sergeant, and Cobbett's regiment followed in 1791. He procured his discharge from the army and at once sought her out. He found her '*a servant of all work* at *five pounds a year* in the house of a Captain Brisac'; on the 5th of February 1792 he married her at Woolwich; and he never had cause to regret the strange fashion in which he had chosen his wife.

Poor Ann! It was an adventurous business being the wife of William Cobbett. The very first thing he did after his marriage was to get himself into such a complicated spider's web of charges and counter-charges that he could only escape from it by fleeing the country. He had the sort of obtrusive downright honesty which always makes trouble for its possessor; and so, as soon as he had secured his discharge from the army, he set about making charges of peculation against certain officers of his regiment. No doubt these accusations were quite well-founded; strictly honest quartermasters were even rarer then than they are to-day. Nevertheless it was silly of Cobbett to prefer particular charges, because the corruption and misappropriation of which he complained were not peculiar to his regiment, but were common to the whole army.

The trouble was that he had the reforming type of mind—which is always a nuisance to constituted authority. He must always be putting things to rights; he could not bear to see the wicked flourishing like the green bay tree. 'If accident had not taken me from the plough, many a villain would have slept at peace by day and swaggered about at night.' Wiser men than Cobbett have not cared very much whether villains sleep at peace or not, so long as those villains do not do *them* any harm; but Cobbett did not possess that sort of tolerance. He was like a man who, abhorring hornets and yet being troubled with no hornets in his own garden, rushes off and attacks a hornets' nest in the garden of one of his neighbours. The motives of such a man may be excellent, but he is often a very troublesome fellow. So was Cobbett, and it is hardly surprising that the Government did its utmost to discourage him from stirring up hornets in its own War Office. But a policy of *laissez aller* was abhorrent to him; he refused to take the Government's hint, he went up to the War Office in person (this ex-sergeant-major of the line, not yet in his thirties!), he worried the life out of the Secretary for War, he appealed direct to Pitt himself, and he even sent a petition to the King. He made himself such a nuisance, in fact, that the Government decided he must be silenced. Plots were hatched against him. Men were brought secretly to London, prepared to swear that he had drunk destruction to the House of Brunswick. Only just in time he realized that he was running his head into a noose; and he showed belated common sense by dropping his charges and fleeing, with Ann at his side, to the little village of Tilques near St. Omer in France.

He stayed there for five months, laboriously perfecting his knowledge of the French language; and he was in a coach on his way to Paris in August 1792 when he heard the first news of the attack on the Tuileries and the deposition of King Louis. He knew that this would mean war between England and France. He dared not return to England, and he could not stay where he was, so he hastened to Le Havre and took ship for America. He landed in October and remained in America for nearly eight years.

At first, things were peaceful enough. Perhaps, in this new strange country, Cobbett could discover no hornets to stir up; perhaps he was merely finding his feet and biding his time and marking down hornets' nests for the future. At any rate, he contented himself for a while with teaching English to French *émigrés* at Philadelphia and with writing *Le Tuteur Anglais,* an English grammar written in French. Ten years ago he had been teaching the rudiments of English grammar to himself; now he was writing a text-book on the subject—in French!

For the faithful Ann, during this brief calm period, life cannot have been so peaceful after all. So terrific was Cobbett's vitality that whether he was writing books on grammar or engaging in furious political controversies he always had plenty to spare for domestic and conjugal affairs. It was during those first years at Philadelphia that he began to procreate children as fast as it was possible for a monogamist to do so.

I have never been able to discover how many children Ann actually bore. Seven survived in-

National Portrait Gallery

WILLIAM COBBETT
(*Painter uncertain*)

fancy: four boys and three girls; but many others were stillborn or died shortly after birth. Ann herself must have been almost as tough as Cobbett; for in these early days, says Cobbett proudly, no servant ever entered his house, though he was well able to afford one. Cleaning, cooking, washing-up, mending and making clothes—Ann did it all; and there can have been very few consecutive months during which she was not pregnant. Poor Ann! Although Cobbett wrote of her affectionately and often, he tells us little of her personality, and she remains a rather dim and shadowy figure, of whom we know nothing save that she must have spent all her days in feeding and clothing Cobbett and Cobbett's children, and that her nights must have been almost as wakeful as her days!

However, if peace can be a relative term, this business of the interminable daily round, pregnancy, labour, and pregnancy again, must have seemed peaceful to Ann when she looked back at it out of the turmoil of later years. Cobbett would never be content for long with the teaching of English and the compilation of uncontroversial grammar-books; he must be hornet-hunting again! So he rushed on to the battlefield of American politics and there, with squibs and lampoons bursting continually about him, with pamphlets raining upon his head like a storm of shrapnel, he was, as we can imagine, happy enough. Like most Radicals, he was intensely patriotic; he loved nothing better than criticizing his own country and abusing his own countrymen, but he would always defend both against criticism and abuse from foreigners. If the British Government was to be baited (and very well it deserved baiting), then he, Cobbett, was the man to do it, and he 'd stand no interference from the citizens of other nations. There is no more scurrilous traducer of England than the English Radical at home, and no more stout-hearted defender of England than the same English Radical abroad. Cobbett was no exception to this rule. Because the American Democrats were strongly pro-French he furiously pamphleteered on the side of the Federalists. He took the pseudonym of 'Peter Porcupine' and, as it were, arched his back and stuck out his quills and challenged the whole city of Philadelphia to attack him. American political controversy, at that time, was no gloved gentlemanly business, and pamphlets with such titles as *A Pill for Peter Porcupine*, *A Roaster for Peter Porcupine*, and so on, were answered by Cobbett with others bearing such aggressive names as *A Kick for a Bite*. There was a tremendous sale for these vigorous, scurrilous, pseudo-philosophical broadsheets, and each Federal salvo provoked a Democratic reply, so that the streets of Philadelphia must have seemed to contain the aftermath of a gigantic paper-chase. But pamphlets, even such slashing pamphlets as these, were mere dust-shot after all, and Cobbett pugnaciously decided that he would provoke something heavier, even if that something turned out to be paving-stones! Accordingly he bought a bookshop and filled it with portraits of all the kings and princes (including, of course, George the Third) who were most obnoxious to the Philadelphian mob. There were angry murmurings from the crowd which filled the street on the day when the bookshop was opened, and there were threats that the windows would be smashed before nightfall; but in the end the mob dispersed, no actual violence was done, and Cobbett had to wait until his return to England before his windows were broken by a mob.

However, he got all the publicity he desired—even to a threat that his house would be burned down. Cobbett was as happy as the day was long. Meanwhile, within the house, Ann (whose first child had died and whose second had been still-born) was placidly giving birth to a daughter.

Cobbett's first residence in America came rather abruptly to an end on the 1st of June 1800, when he sailed for home and sent an Open Letter to the principal American papers which characteristically began: 'When people care not two straws for each other, ceremony at parting is mere grimace. . . .' He was feeling very sore, and the chief reason for his feeling of soreness was that in the previous year he had been fined five thousand dollars for libel.

It was hardly to be expected that Cobbett would keep out of serious trouble for long. He had written a score of violent pamphlets, he had filled his bookshop with the most inflammatory literature, he had played upon political hatreds until he had the whole city of Philadelphia thirsting for his blood; and when he began to publish a daily paper, *Porcupine's Gazette,* in which he said exactly and unequivocally what he thought about his various enemies, it was certain that sooner or later he would overstep the mark. And indeed, *Porcupine's Gazette* had not been in existence for more than a month or two before its editor was served with writs for libel upon the Spanish Minister and the King of Spain. Luckily for him the Grand Jury threw out the bill against him by a majority of one; and Cobbett, instead of thanking his stars for the escape and walking more warily in the future, wrote a furious pamphlet denouncing the chief justice, Thomas M'Kean.

His next case did not end so fortunately. It happened that America was visited by a bad epidemic of yellow fever, for which the favourite treatment was that invented by a Dr. Rush—a treatment consisting of copious bleedings and equally copious dosings with 'mercurial purgings' known as 'Rush's Powders.' Now Dr. Benjamin Rush was one of the leaders of the Democratic Party, and no doubt it seemed to Cobbett that any stick would serve with which to belabour such a man. Therefore, in several successive issues of *Porcupine's Gazette,* he savagely attacked both Dr. Rush and his famous powders: as palpable a libel as was ever committed. Dr. Rush's action against him lasted two years, but eventually Cobbett was fined five thousand dollars by the new Chief Justice, Shippen, who was a Democrat and a friend of M'Kean. In the circumstances Cobbett appears to have got off lightly; one hesitates to suppose what damages a modern English court would give for such a libel.

Exceedingly angry and — strangely enough — genuinely surprised, Cobbett shook the dust of Philadelphia off his feet and moved to New York, where he worked off steam by publishing a new fortnightly paper called the *Rushlight,* which was wholly devoted to an attack upon his latest enemy. It contained an almost interminable argument against the doctor's treatment of yellow fever, admixed with an equally voluminous diatribe against the wretched man's political opinions; and it had also a full account of the trial, with a number of acid comments upon the Chief Justice and his friendship with M'Kean. This extraordinary magazine only lasted for five numbers; after which, presumably, Cobbett could find nothing more to say about Dr. Rush.

Meanwhile, his position in America had become precarious. His Philadelphian property and stock-in-trade had been sold up, he was financially embarrassed, and he was living under the continual threat of deportation. He was very angry with America, and he decided to leave it; so he left his New York business in reliable hands and set sail for England—though not before he had gleefully pointed out that George Washington, the President, was dying under Dr. Rush's treatment for the yellow fever.

His eight years in America had been eventful enough, and already his writings had earned him a reputation. The sly Talleyrand, sojourning in America, had thought him worth a visit—and had received from Cobbett a characteristic rebuff. The British Government, through its agents, had offered him money in return for his services—which he had refused. England was prepared to honour her innkeeper's son who had so stoutly defended her good name in a far land. Cobbett's homecoming was almost triumphant. He was asked to edit a Government newspaper. Honours and a fortune might have been his. The people loved him; he was a picturesque and popular figure already. But alas! he had the Radical mind. Abroad, he would defend the rulers of England against the faintest whisper of criticism; at home, he would never be happy unless he were violently opposed to those same rulers. He must be 'agin the Government,' he must be for ever attacking those in authority, he must be thoroughly unpopular, and then he would be content. . . .

It took him rather more than a year to dissipate the warm welcoming atmosphere which had surrounded him at his homecoming. In October 1801 London was illuminated in honour of the French envoy and in celebration of the peace with France. Cobbett, who had opposed the peace, was prepared to sit up all night in darkness rather than allow a gleam of acquiescing candlelight to shine through *his* windows; and so, while every other house showed a dozen little beacons in honour of the general joy, the windows of No. 11 Pall Mall stared blankly, darkly, and disapprovingly upon the scene, a silent protest which was altogether too much for the excited mob. Every window in the house was broken (no doubt to Cobbett's huge delight) and the front door was forced open before the rioters were dispersed. Ann, meanwhile, was in the throes of another confinement. . . .

These scenes were re-enacted six months later, when the Treaty of Amiens was formally ratified. Once more the crowd smashed Cobbett's dark windows which seemed to frown with puritanical disapproval upon the scene of their merrymaking; and this time a troop of Horse Guards had to be called before the mob would go away.

Cobbett's next venture was the publication of the *Political Register*, which in 1803 cost him £1,000 in damages in connection with two actions instituted by the Government and the Solicitor-General for Ireland respectively. Nevertheless the paper was a huge success, and it was destined to continue upon its merry way, attacking almost everybody and almost everything, until Cobbett's death in 1835. It began with the most impeccable high Tory principles and it ended as a vigorous exponent of reform; but it remained throughout an expression of Cobbett's essentially Radical personality, and it mirrored the mind of its editor more plainly than any other newspaper—except perhaps the *Manchester Guardian* under C. P. Scott—has done before or since.

In 1802 Cobbett's Radicalism was expressing

itself in a rather curious way. He was furiously denouncing the French Revolution, opposing the peace with France, and loudly beating the drums of war. Later, his opinion on all these matters was to change; for the moment, he was 'agin the Government,' and that was all that mattered. He was also busily attacking Pitt's Funding System, the growth of the national debt, and the rise of the new class of stock-jobbing parasites and 'all the innumerable swarm of locusts who, without stirring ten miles from the capital, devour three-fourths of the produce of the whole land.' This was more in keeping with his later principles; but in curious contrast he was also opposing the Bill for the suppression of bear-baiting (a Bill which he considered to be an unwarrantable interference with the manly sports of the British people), the abolition of the Slave Trade, and the freedom of the Press (except where his own freedom was concerned). He mocked impartially at all the enthusiasts who desired 'the converting of negroes into saints; Sunday schools for making scholars of those whose business it is to delve; soup kitchens for feeding those who are too idle to work and too proud to beg; thick handkerchieves for ladies' bosoms . . .' and so on. He jeered, in fact, at all reformers—he who was to be the arch-priest of reform; and yet, perhaps, there was less inconsistency in this than at first appears. As a matter of fact there is in Cobbett's life and writing a sort of consistency which is far deeper rooted than any mere adherence to a party or a principle. He was always consistent to himself. His opinions upon this subject or that might change and change again, but he remained throughout an English peasant, one might almost say a personification of the whole English peasantry, possessing all their ancient prejudices, putting into words the love of the things they loved mutely, and speaking on their behalf, without much thought and without regard for reason or doctrine, their older wisdom, which is the wisdom of the heart. Thus, though he might give this or that reason for his support of the war with France, he was really, I believe, expressing the long enmity of the men whose forefathers had fought with Henry V at Agincourt. When he attacked money and manufactures he was merely clothing in argument the instinctive mistrust of all countrymen for the two things which they knew (without understanding the why and wherefore) were destined to be their deadliest foes. And when he supported bull-baiting, he was giving voice to the legitimate fear of the peasant-folk that when this old liberty was taken away from them, others would swiftly follow it. Even freedom to torture a beast may be a symbol of a wider freedom; and though Cobbett did not say so, he must have guessed that the voices which condemned the sport of bull-baiting as barbarous and cruel would soon be condemning the fox-hunt and the hare-hunt for the same reasons, would be deploring the maypole as a phallic symbol and the old country feasts as licentious and pagan. For Macaulay said a very true thing when he said that the Puritans objected to bear-baiting, not because it gave pain to the bear, but because it gave pleasure to the spectators.

Even in Philadelphia, even in London, in the whirl of politics and pamphlets, Cobbett had remained the English countryman; and now, in 1805, the land which he loved more than anything else in the world called him back again, and he bought a farm called Fairthorn on the River Hamble at Botley, about five miles from Southampton. Here he settled down, close enough to London to enable him to continue his political and journalistic activities. In his spare time he farmed and planted trees—what a typically English delight that is!—while Ann managed the big farm-house and bore more children. (It must have seemed quite strange to Ann that her labours were no longer accompanied by the yells of the mob and the breaking of windows!)

Miss Mitford, the author of *Our Village*, makes a pleasant picture out of her visit to the Botley household. The house itself was large, massive, red and square, and perched on a considerable eminence—'not unlike its proprietor,' says Miss Mitford, with a spice of friendly mischief. The hospitality was simple and genuine. 'There was not the slightest attempt at finery, display, or gentility. They called it a farm-house, and everything was in accordance with the largest idea of a great English yeoman of the time. Everything was excellent, everything abundant—all served with the greatest nicety by trim waiting-damsels; and everything went on with such quiet regularity, that of the large circle of guests not one could find himself in the way.'

Ann must have been a very wonderful woman. Not only did she contrive efficiently to manage this big household during the intervals between her confinements, but she also looked after all her children (she must have begun to feel like the old woman who lived in a shoe!), and even gave lessons to her daughters—for it happened that one of Cobbett's chief prejudices was against schools, particularly schools for girls. Yet she was 'a sweet motherly woman,' says Miss Mitford, likening her to Scott's Ailie Dinmont—simple and kind, and devoted to her husband and her children.

Cobbett himself was 'a tall, stout man, fair, and sunburnt, with a bright smile, and an air compounded of the soldier and the farmer, to which his habit of wearing an eternal red waistcoat contributed not a little.' He still possessed enough energy for twenty men. He was busy with a hundred things in London (in 1806 he definitely went over to the Radical Party, and stood for Honiton as anti-bribery candidate in a by-election) and yet he still had time to assist at his haymaking and harvest, to promote single-stick competitions among his labourers, to plant trees and mow his lawn before breakfast, and finally—how like Cobbett!—to engage in a furious quarrel with the Reverend Mr. Baker, the Botley parson.

Tranquillity would have no place in Cobbett's heaven; and although everything seems to have been idyllic in the village of Botley, there was a sweet peacefulness about the place which, no doubt, he found extremely distasteful. Seeking an antagonist, he found an almost perfect one in the person of the unfortunate Mr. Baker. In the first place he disliked the poor man's sermons and 'longed to horsewhip him in the pulpit for talking such nonsense'; in the second place, the two disagreed over village affairs; and in the third, there was (and still is) a good old tradition in

English village life that the squire or chief yeoman should quarrel with the parson.

The row began with several minor clashes, which developed into open war over some observations about parsons in general which Cobbett had seen fit to publish in the *Register*. After that, I am afraid, Cobbett simply persecuted the poor man, whose incumbency seems to have been pretty turbulent anyhow, since he frequently came to blows with the village doctor, who on one occasion horsewhipped him and on another engaged in fisticuffs with him in his own vestry. Cobbett's persecution lasted many years and took many forms. He called Mr. Baker 'an abominable liar' in public, at which the assembled villagers wildly cheered. He wrote epigrams about him and called him offensive names. He even broke into poetry—a rare thing for Cobbett—the better to express his loathing for one whom he likened to a magpie:

> Of all the birds, this prying pest
> Must needs be parson o'er the rest.

Elsewhere he called him 'a greedy, chattering, lying, backbiting, mischief-making, everlasting plague.' He was always prodigal of invective, but he never exhausted his store; for he persecuted Mr. Baker without intermission till the end of his days, and did not even forget him when he was sent to prison in 1810. Hearing that in his absence Ann and Mr. Baker had patched up the quarrel, he wrote urgently from Newgate begging her to have nothing to do with such a rogue.

Cobbett was too plain-spoken to keep out of prison for ever. Too often for the peace of mind of those in authority he had demanded leave to speak his mind and had not troubled to put on his motley before he did so. There was never a quality of 'fun' or mocking in his controversial writings; his method was the method of one who bangs people over the head with a single-stick. In 1810 he elected to beat the Government over the head in connection with the flogging of some soldiers at Ely. His article in the *Political Register* was considered to be subversive; he was found guilty of sedition, and sentenced to two years' imprisonment with a fine of a thousand pounds. He received his sentence with a smile, and was immediately carried to Newgate, whence he continued to direct his affairs and edit the *Political Register* with undiminished courage. In some of the bravest phrases ever written in the English language, he declared that the court had passed no sentence of imprisonment upon his mind.

With this splendid affirmation he set himself to face the two long years in Newgate jail.

He did not forget Fairthorn during those years; paradoxically, indeed, the farm seemed closer to him now that he could no longer visit it. A man in confinement will always think most about that which he loves most, and Cobbett's thoughts during his imprisonment were chiefly of Botley and his children, who still lived there. Every week there came to Newgate prison a hamper of Fairthorn produce: eggs from his own hens, fresh butter from his own cows, fruit from his own orchards, with perhaps a few ears of wheat or barley tucked away in a corner, so that he could see what good stuff still came out of the Hampshire land. There would be a little bundle of letters too—one every week from every child—and there would be the weekly journal, compiled by the boys and neatly bound, containing a full account of the labours on the farm, the plantings and reapings, the purchases and sales, so that Cobbett, in his prison cell, might know precisely which fields were lying fallow, which grew roots and which grew corn, which were grazed and which were mown—almost as if he were able to be there in person.

And every week he answered each letter scrupulously, and directed the labours of the next week, and thanked James or John for a handful of meadow grasses plucked at haytime or little Eleanour and Susan for a bunch of primroses gathered from a bank beside the River Hamble.

As for Ann, she would be content with no mere hamper-sending and letter-writing; she must be at her husband's side. Although she was in her usual condition of pregnancy, she came up to London as soon as he was sentenced and visited him during his first evening at Newgate. She took lodgings close at hand, and her confinement took place there. The child died.

After that she spent part of her time with the children at Botley and part at Newgate with her husband. When she was away from him Cobbett wrote to her constantly, not of business and the farm, but of personal, intimate things. He would entreat her not to worry about him, or beg her half-humorously not to wear so much flannel. 'Pray, do leave off some of it. It rubs you, and it scrubs you, all to pieces. . . . I do not like to see you with *waistcoats* and *breastplates*; but the *Breeches* is the worst of all. Now, pray, mind what I say, about these nasty Breeches.'

On the 8th of July 1812 Cobbett wrote his last article from prison, gaily subscribing beneath it the words: 'State Prison, Newgate, where I have just paid a thousand pounds fine to the King; and much good may it do his Majesty.' Two days later he returned to Botley, where he was enthusiastically greeted by the villagers. One thing only marred the reception: there was no peal of bells, because Mr. Baker, who was in the middle of another furious controversy with Cobbett upon the subject of Thomas Paine's deistical *Age of Reason,* refused point-blank to hand over the keys of the church. However, the villagers made up for the unwelcoming silence of the bells by taking the horses out of Cobbett's carriage and dragging him in triumph from Botley to Fairthorn.

It must have been a joyous homecoming. There was the square red-brick farm-house, open-faced and full of greeting, there were the orchards with their burden of little apples, there was the mown hay sweet-smelling in the meadows, cocks and swaths behind which the children hid themselves, there was the meadowsweet in the hedgerow, the honeysuckle and the wild rose. And all his children running to greet him; and Ann, placid, smiling, homely, and not quite so bundled up with flannel underclothes (we may suppose), because it was summer-time.

And all the villagers, all those good sound solid farm-labourers, who worked for him and for whom he worked so unceasingly, turned out with their wives to bid him welcome! What a blessed day! And there was not one single fly in the ointment; for the Botley parson, damned magpie, churlishly kept within doors and would take no part in the rejoicing. Good, good. . . . It was nice to find that everything was the same as it had been before!

Fairthorn must have seemed a very blissful place to Cobbett during those five years after he came out of Newgate jail. Yet because of the fierce reforming restlessness that was in him, he could not be content to enjoy Fairthorn and live at peace with the world. Once again he threw his colossal energies into politics. He stood for Parliament at Southampton and was defeated; and he strenuously opposed the General Enclosure Bill of 1813 (the English peasant again, fighting for his ancient common rights!). Chiefly, however, he concentrated on the question of reform, using all the authority and influence of the *Political Register* on the side of the agitators. At that time there was a strange restive spirit abroad in England. Not even the drums of Waterloo could drown the voices of those who cried, not for victories, but for a new freedom. This awakening spirit manifested itself in the activities of a number of small reforming societies, many of which were directed by cranks and crooks, and some of which were dedicated to violence. Cobbett had a wider vision, and he was not greatly in sympathy with these tendencies: he saw that they were unimportant. The Government, however, was either stampeded into believing them dangerous, or it determined to make them the excuse for another attack upon free speech, aimed, not only at them, but at Cobbett himself. On the 4th of March 1817 the Habeas Corpus Act was suspended, and 'agitators' became liable to imprisonment without trial. Cobbett knew exactly what this meant. He acted swiftly and wisely. He went secretly to Liverpool, and, on the 27th of March, he sailed for the second time to the United States. He was not running away because he was afraid; he was leaving because he knew that if he remained he would very soon find himself in prison, where he would be of little use. From America he could continue to edit the *Political Register*, and his voice would still be heard in England.

It must have hurt him to leave Fairthorn, at a time when the corn was coming up on the ploughlands.

As soon as he reached America, Cobbett began to look for a farm. He was like a hardy plant which, being transplanted to a new situation, immediately sets about getting its roots into the soil. Cobbett must always be soundly rooted, and the farm which he rented at North Hempsted was the next best thing to Fairthorn.

The labour of putting the land and house in order would have been quite sufficient to occupy an ordinary man; but Cobbett added to it the troublesome and difficult business of editing the *Political Register* from a distance of several thousand miles. Every week he dispatched his vigorous, characteristic 'copy' to London, where it appeared about two months later, having lost little of its freshness in the journey. In addition he found time to write three books: a treatise on gardening, a brilliant *Grammar of the English Language,* and a strange and delightful work entitled *A Journal of a Year's Residence in the United States.*

This last book is very characteristic of Cobbett. It is a curious mixture of diary, farming handbook, and political treatise. It is almost fantastically digressive. A considerable part of it is devoted to an account of the proper cultivation of the Swedish turnip; in the middle of which occurs a tremendous homily against drinking. A little earlier we have a furious denunciation of the potato, 'a noxious weed' and 'a root worse than useless'; and mixed up with this diatribe is a condemnation of Milton for the faulty theology of his *Paradise Lost* and of Shakespeare for his 'bombast, puns, and smut.' There were no half-measures about Cobbett's judgments. When he was right, he was devastatingly right; when he was wrong, he succeeded in being more completely wrong than one would believe it possible for a sensible man to be.

What with farming, English politics, the compilation of grammars, and the praise of his beloved swedes, Cobbett's two years in America were pretty full ones; and he contrived to make time also to engage in a violent quarrel with one Thomas Fearon, who had the temerity to state in print that Cobbett's American residence was 'mouldering into decay.' The wretched man had meant no harm; he had, indeed, been moved to pity at Cobbett's surroundings—'a path rarely trod, fences in ruins, the gate broken. . . .' Whether or not the account was true, it infuriated Cobbett, who wanted no man's pity, so he wrote and published a whole pamphlet called *Fearon's Falsehoods* in order to refute it. This trivial quarrel added a spice to Cobbett's residence in America; two years without a row would have been too dull altogether.

Nor was the Botley parson forgotten. Cobbett might be thousands of miles away from him, but he would not let him rest. In 1817 he sent to the *Political Register* an article upon tithes in which he compared English parsons most unfavourably with American ones. 'Why cannot you reverence God,' he wrote, 'without Baker and his wife and children eating up a tenth part of the corn and milk and eggs and lambs and pigs and calves that are produced in Botley parish!' Poor Mr. Baker! Cobbett must have seemed omnipresent, like the devil himself. There was no respite from him.

In 1818 the period of suspension of the Habeas Corpus Act ended. It would be safe now for Cobbett to return to England. But he was busy with his books and he did not do so at once—he waited until the following year, when by some ill-chance his house caught fire and was burned to the ground. Nothing ordinary ever happened to Cobbett; his exits and his entrances must always be violent and spectacular, and on the only occasion when Cobbett himself failed to arrange a dramatic departure the elements assisted him. No quiet, unheralded comings and goings would be his; if he were not fleeing from the law, or escaping from a plot, or sweeping out in a furious temper, then nothing less than an Act of God should speed him!

And as if the flames leaping high over North Hempsted farm were not enough to make his exit sensational, he must needs associate with his departure the most extraordinary action of his career. In his early days he had grossly libelled the character of Tom Paine, the author of *The Age of Reason* and *The Rights of Man*; he had since become converted to some of Paine's opinions, and he was anxious to make amends. Now Paine had died in America and, as a deist, had been denied Christian burial. Cobbett saw an opportunity of atoning for his scurrilous pamphlet, so he went to New Rochelle, where Paine's body was buried in unhallowed ground, and got leave to dig it up. When he took ship to England (in October 1819) he carried the coffin with him, and after a good deal of trouble with the Customs he brought it ashore at Liverpool.

But alas! his homecoming from America was not so triumphant as it had been last time. Cobbett and the coffin were greeted with ridicule. And nobody wanted the bones of Tom Paine, nor were the necessary funds forthcoming to build a mausoleum for them. They remained in Cobbett's possession until his death, and passed to his eldest son, after which they disappeared and were lost for ever.

Cobbett returned to an unrestful England. There was unemployment in the cities and acute distress in the country districts. The agitation for reform was growing every day. Half the popular leaders were in prison or on bail awaiting trial. In Saint Peter's Fields at Manchester a great meeting had been dispersed by the yeomanry in such a manner that the event became known as 'the Peterloo massacre.' There was plenty of work for Cobbett, and he threw himself into the turmoil straight away. He addressed a huge concourse at Liverpool and went on to Manchester; but Manchester was an armed camp, and the authorities forbade him to enter it. Going on to Coventry, he addressed another meeting and was turned out of his hotel. He made his way to London through a torrent of abuse, and at London he was at once arrested for an old debt, and had to be bailed out by two of his friends.

But this was the sort of rough-and-tumble life that Cobbett enjoyed. There were hard knocks to be taken and hard knocks to be given, and very merrily he entered the fight. He published a new daily newspaper, which disastrously failed; and he unsuccessfully fought a rather violent election at Coventry. These two expensive ventures between them effected his financial ruin, and in 1820 he was compelled to file his petition in bankruptcy. In the same year he was involved in two more libel actions; and he also quarrelled furiously with his publisher, Benbow, just as he had earlier quarrelled with his previous publisher, Wright. He filled what was left of a very exciting year with a stout championship of the chastity of Queen Caroline, whose affairs, and those of the new king, George IV, were causing a major political scandal.

We may suppose that Cobbett was thoroughly happy in the midst of all these alarums. So long as he was able to lay about him in his own defence, let disasters fall upon him thick and fast; he didn't care! The only misfortune which really grieved him was the loss of Fairthorn Farm, caused by his bankruptcy. The farm in America had never been more than a poor substitute for Botley, to which he had been looking forward to return. In America, he complained, the flowers were without scent and the birds without song. He missed the Hampshire violets and the blackbirds, and the redbreast's Christmas carol. In short, he was an Englishman in exile, longing for English things. Now he returned home, and that which he loved most was wrested from him by his creditors. Those orchards which he had so carefully tended, those ploughlands which grew such good wheat and barley, those oak trees which he had planted with his own hands that his grandchildren might enjoy their shade—these were his no longer. And there were no more welcomes from the good friendly villagers, no more Christmas dinners in the great red-brick farm-house, no more parochial quarrels with the infamous Botley parson. . . . A chapter was ended.

But Cobbett was never one to let misfortune down him. 'They have now, they say, *sunk* me in good earnest,' he wrote at the time. 'Never was a man so often sunk! This is not sinking! This is what the sailors call merely "*shipping a sea.*"' He might heel over, but he'd right himself very soon; and because it was essential to his own stability that he should be rooted, he took a small house at Kensington, with four acres of good lands for cows and pigs and extensive nursery gardens surrounding it. Here, in the midst of all his hard work in the cause of reform, he amused himself by developing a little seed farm, in which he grew such American importations as acacia trees, and maize, which he called 'Cobbett's Corn,' and—inevitably—his favourite swedes. Here too he wrote a book on horse-hoeing, a treatise on arboriculture, an account of the cultivation of maize, and a nondescript work called *Cottage Economy* '*containing information relative to the brewing of Beer, making of Bread, keeping of Cows, Pigs, Bees, Ewes, Goats, Poultry, and Rabbits, and relative to other matters deemed useful in the conducting of the affairs of a labourer's family; to which are added, instructions relative to the selecting, the cutting, and the bleaching of the Plants of English Grass and Grain, for the purpose of making Hats and Bonnets; and also instructions for the erecting and using Bee-houses after the Virginian manner.'* In spite of its unwieldy list of contents, the book is a model of practicality and good writing. Cobbett could make even the manufacture of straw bonnets interesting. And, being Cobbett, he was as digressive as ever. The chapter in which he praised the virtues of beer contained a long and savage diatribe against tea, which was just then coming into fashion. And just as no subject was too big for him to tackle, so was nothing too small to claim his attention; indeed, he even set himself to improve the domestic fire-grate, writing an article upon it in the *Political Register* and including a full-page illustration of his new design!

Meanwhile, to add the usual spice to existence, he attacked impartially the writers of religious tracts, such as Hannah More (whom he termed the 'Old Bishop in petticoats'), and the advocates of birth control, such as Carlile and 'the monster Malthus.' Throughout his life, he was never short of *somebody* to beat over the head.

The years between 1820 and 1832 were troubled

and turbulent. Politically, all was confusion; Parliament consisted of a succession of dog-fights. Socially, they were years of alternate rioting and repression. Fear was in all men's hearts. The ruling classes were desperately afraid of revolution, which has probably never seemed so near in England; the labourers were afraid of the machines which threatened them with a new bondage, and of the hoofs of the soldiers' horses, which had trampled them down at Peterloo. In many respects the times resembled our own: crisis followed crisis, there were runs on the banks, and the solid foundation of things seemed to have vanished. Cobbett was well into his sixties; and it was not, one would suppose, an old man's world. Yet he hurled himself into the turmoil and for twelve years fought harder than ever in the cause of reform. In 1826 (being then sixty-two) he fought an unruly election at Preston, which he afterwards described as the happiest time of his life, except that of his marriage. In the course of this election he was hustled by a mob, and the *Morning Herald* aroused his fury by expressing its concern that 'an old man' should have been treated so. 'An *old man,*' observed Cobbett angrily, 'let Thwaites of the *Morning Herald* recollect, who could catch him by one of those things that he calls his legs, and toss him over the fence from Piccadilly into the

Green Park.' As if to prove this, in the following year he was involved in a free fight at a public dinner.

During all these years, whenever he could spare the time away from London, he rode out on extensive tours throughout the country, lecturing to the labourers and writing the journal which formed the basis of his most famous book, *Rural Rides*. As Mr. F. E. Green pointed out, it is the book of a man who talks at the top of his voice; but shouting is not offensive in the open air. And it is a great book, because Cobbett knew exactly what he was shouting about. The quality of the ploughing, the Wiltshire cornfields, the cattle and sheep in the pastures, the turnips and the swedes: these were the things which Cobbett noticed as he rode his twenty or thirty miles a day through the south-country villages. Because he so well understood the soil, he wrote supremely well about it; *Rural Rides* is great because it is written from the heart. It has a splendid quality of spontaneity; Cobbett always writes down what he is thinking at the moment. All his wild prejudices are there, his prejudices against tea and drinking and religious tracts, but they have become familiar to us, and we regard them almost affectionately, as we regard the well-known eccentricities of a loved friend. And all his good sound sensible convictions are there too, spoken fearlessly at the top of his voice. His pleasure at the sight of some fine fat cattle is spoiled by the thought that the Jews and the stock-jobbers will probably eat them; but he likes to see good crops and plenty of stock in the fields, because this confounds the abominable theories of the monster Malthus, who says that unless the poor restrict their breeding there won't be enough for everybody to eat. Damned nonsense! says Cobbett. However, so long as a tenth of the produce goes in tithes, no wonder the labourers are hungry. Whenever he passes the prosperous-looking house of a village parson Cobbett casts a hostile glance at it: and even the black-coated rooks on the stubbles remind him of the parsons; only *they* have more right to a tithe of the wheat than the clergy have!

Thus breezily Cobbett rides on. And he is not always denouncing evil—he finds plenty of good things in the countryside as well. He notes with appreciation the prettiness of the girls in Sussex and in the Kent marches; he asks a handsome gipsy to tell his fortune at Tichborne; he approves the sport of foxhunting; he is delighted to see a crop of 'Cobbett's Corn'; he declares that the squire at Witley is one that England should be proud of because he knows how to plant trees.

He goes to Botley, a queer, rather wistful re-visiting; but the turnips are a good crop there (and so they ought to be, since he has taught the farmers how to grow them), and the trees which he planted with his own hands are growing well. For old times' sake he rides up to the house of Mr. Baker in the hope of getting a glimpse of him; but although he bellows and cracks his whip under the miserable man's windows, he will not budge, and Cobbett goes away disappointed. He would have liked to have another row.

But that is merely an amusing interlude. There are things of much greater moment to concern him in his beloved countryside than the delinquencies of the Botley parson: the Rotten Boroughs, and the 'whiskered gentry' who own the land yet have no real connection with it, the wretched, half-starved labourers, the girls working in the fields 'as pale as ashes, and as ragged as colts.' These things make Cobbett passionately angry; he loves the land of England too much to be able to bear to see it misused so. As he rides back to London he predicts that soon the silent suffering people will rise; hunger will drive them to it. That was the spring of 1830. In the next autumn the ricks began to blaze across the south country, the bright beacons in one village were a signal to the next, and thus the poor dumb ragged folk that had never spoken for their rights before spoke for them now as best they knew how—in fire.

In 1831 Cobbett was once more tried for sedition; but this time not even a packed jury would convict. Cobbett conducted his own defence, and spoke admirably for four and a half hours. The jury disagreed, and the Government made no attempt at a second trial. The tide had turned.

On the 7th of July 1832 the Reform Bill at last became an Act.

George IV, whom Cobbett had heartily hated, had died in 1830, and Cobbett, in the *Register*, had performed a sort of war-dance over his grave. 'On a review of his whole life,' he wrote, 'I can find no one good thing to speak of, in either the conduct or character of this king.' Cobbett had rejoiced in the same way over the deaths of Pitt and Castlereagh. Forgiveness was not one of his virtues. 'I have not so read the Holy Scriptures,' he once declared, 'I have not, from them, learned that I am not to rejoice at the fall of unjust foes.' Cobbett was never a gentleman; he was something much more engaging.

The passing of the Reform Bill, which swept away the Rotten Boroughs and considerably increased the franchise, was the culmination of Cobbett's life work. But it was not like him to rest upon his oars. At Michaelmas, 1832, he acquired a long lease of Normandy Farm at Ash, Surrey (not far from his birthplace, Farnham), characteristically declaring: 'A farmer I will live and die.' In December of the same year he was elected Member of Parliament for Oldham. He combined his farming activities with hard work in the House of Commons, agitating for the Shorter Working Day and opposing the new Poor Laws. He also continued his riding tours of the countryside, even visiting North Wales and Ireland, where he had plenty of opportunities for denouncing those 'ever-damned potatoes.' He returned home in the spring of 1835, full of plans for a new daily newspaper, for improvements to his farm, and for his future writings. He went down to Ash and heard the cuckoo in April, which was earlier than he had ever heard it before. He would have liked to spend all his time at Normandy Farm, but parliamentary business took him to London, where he fell ill. When he returned to the country he was a sick man. He caught a chill through imprudently drinking tea in the open air (Mr. G. D. H. Cole observes: 'How are the mighty fallen!') and became so seriously ill that it was apparent to his family that he was dying. He asked that he might be carried out into the fields, so that he might see how the work was progressing, and this was done; he wished for 'four days' rain' for the Cobbett's Corn and the swedes; and this was almost his last wish, for that night he died.

That famous newspaper which had no cause to love him and which he had called 'the bloody, bloody old *Times*,' declared at his death that he had been an English episode and nothing more; but it added, not ungenerously, that he was a more extraordinary Englishman than any other of his time, and that he was a man whom England alone could have produced. Certainly it is difficult to imagine a French or German or American Cobbett; and I think one may say that, had he been any other countryman but our own, he would have been no more than a phenomenon; he would have accomplished nothing. He might have lived in history as a glorious eccentric—'some comet or unusual prodigy'; as a literary curiosity, as a creature of wild humours, or even as a most memorable, superlative, and stupendous fool. Some out-of-the-way corner, some nook or cranny of history, would in any case have been his; but I think he would never have been allowed to exercise his influence on history, in any country other than our own.

I suppose it is only because we are English that we have taken Cobbett seriously; and in saying that I do not intend to belittle Cobbett, I do not mean that he was not eminently worthy of being taken seriously. But the fact remains that he was so extraordinary a person that he might well have become a sort of national joke. All his life he sailed close to the wind of comedy; and when one is reading about him one often has that slightly uncomfortable feeling which one experiences when somebody is telling risky stories in the wrong sort of company. 'Sooner or later he will go too far.' This is the effect produced in me by a biography of Cobbett. 'Sooner or later,' I say, 'this man will make a colossal fool of himself.' Again and again those great gusts of comedy seem likely to capsize him — as when he comes home from America solemnly bearing the disinterred bones of Tom Paine. Time after time he heels over, but somehow or other he rights himself in our eyes and saves himself, by the narrowest of margins, from becoming a clown. Instead of being a national joke, he is very nearly a national prophet; but whether that is due to his genius, or whether it is merely because we are what we are, I cannot certainly decide.

Perhaps the secret of it is that Cobbett's particular form of eccentricity fits in, somehow, with the queer pattern of our national character. He is part of the patchwork—of that fantastic, comic, beautiful patchwork which makes up English life and English history and English literature and English manners. Perhaps his own contribution to it is a little more preposterous than the rest of the patchwork, but it is nevertheless—how shall I put it?—*in the right manner.* It is never alien nor strange, and we understand it because we are slightly preposterous ourselves.

For Cobbett, most changeable in his opinions, could never change himself; and he was ever an English farmer, with the good sound sense, the illogical prejudices, the wooden-headed stupidities, the pugnacity, the John-Bullish obstinacy of an English farmer. All these things were exaggerated in him, but nothing was radically changed—indeed, one might say that he was Radical chiefly in that he was thoroughly rooted in the soil. In his later years he became a sort of colossus, and his prejudices, his stupidity, his pugnacity grew side by side with his good sense. He blew gustily about the world, he blustered into politics, he roared into controversies, but he still did everything in the manner of a south-country farmer going to market. His good sense was the good sense of a man who knows what sort of fertilizer he should use on a particular sort of soil; his prejudices were the age-old prejudices which have always made our agricultural classes so difficult to deal with—the kind which consist of a grain of great wisdom mixed up with a heap of foolishness; and his prose weapon in controversy was rather like a stout ash-plant carried to settle an argument with a trespassing ne'er-do-well. In fact, Cobbett the writer and Cobbett the politician, though they ranged over half the world instead of a few hundred acres, were never essentially different from Cobbett the Hampshire farmer, who quarrelled with the Botley parson and grew such excellent crops of swedes.

Chapter 9 — *The Wind on the Heath*

THOUGH he ranged far and wide over the face of England, Cobbett always had his roots in the Hampshire land. He belonged. Even when he was in France or America he remained the south-country farmer, reluctantly and with many reservations following the maxim: 'When in Rome, do as the Romans do.'

But George Borrow, as picaresque, as polemical, as disputatious as Cobbett, differed from him in one important particular: he had no roots anywhere. He belonged to no country or countryside, no little loved patch of England was his. True, he was born in Norfolk, and spent some years of his later life there; yet there is nothing in his personality or works that would lead one to label him a Norfolk man. Indeed, labels of any sort will not attach to him. He blew about the world, rootless, hearthless, vagabond; a mere wind on the heath.

Perhaps his parentage had something to do with it. His mother was an actress in a travelling theatrical company, and his father a military officer who spent his life posting to and fro between innumerable garrison towns. George Borrow was their second child, and he was born on the 5th of July in the year 1803. He always insisted that his birthplace was East Dereham in Norfolk; he did this partly because he was throughout his life an inveterate liar and partly, we may suppose, because his real birthplace bore the rather ridiculous name of Dumpling Green.

During his childhood he was buffeted from barrack to barrack all over England, moving to and fro in obedience to whatever strange laws governed the orbit of his father's duties. Captain Borrow never stayed anywhere for long, and he seems to have been in many respects a very peculiar man. His claim to fame rests on a somewhat apocryphal tale (told by himself) that he once fought and beat one Big Ben Brain, the greatest prize-fighter of his day. Still more remarkable is his assertion that he later converted Big Ben Brain to the study of the Bible, which he read aloud to him as he lay a-dying. However, both stories may be true, for the Scriptures and the Fancy were the ruling passions of Captain Borrow's life, and an association of the two at

Ben Brain's death-bed would certainly have been to his taste. His piety (in both matters) was very great, and doubtless he instructed his son George, with fine impartiality, in the dynasties of prize-fighters and the somewhat similar-sounding dynasties of the Israelite kings. In his later days, however, deciding that it was impossible to serve both God and Mammon, he eschewed the prize-fighters and fell into a kind of religious gloom; and mention in his presence of the name of Big Ben Brain was strictly forbidden.

George Borrow went to school at Edinburgh and Norwich, and was subsequently articled to a lawyer in the latter town. But he was too restless to content himself for long with such a sedate occupation; he stayed in the office for five years (during which, in his spare time, he feverishly studied languages) and then he went off to London, determined to earn his living by his pen. He proudly carried with him a bundle of translations of Danish and Welsh poetry and an introduction to a publisher, Sir Richard Phillips. Sir Richard, who seems to have been a sensible man if a hard one, suggested to him that he could scarcely expect to make a living by translating poetry, and he had much better write a piece of evangelical trash like *The Dairyman's Daughter*, which was having a great success at the time. Borrow failed to jump at the idea, so Sir Richard set him to work on a series of books called *Celebrated Trials*; and for some time he hunted through the *Newgate Calendar* and other sources for records of the most unpleasant and sensational crimes. He did other hack-work too, including a little reviewing; but when he failed to translate into German Sir Richard's own life-work, which was called *Twelve Essays on the Proximate Causes*, Sir Richard decided that he was ill-equipped for the profession of letters, and dispensed with his services.

For the next eight years Borrow wandered about rather aimlessly, wrote little, and was very poor; we know practically nothing about this period of his life. But in 1833, on the strength of his wide knowledge of languages, he obtained a post with the Bible Society, who sent him to St. Petersburg to superintend the printing of the Bible in the Manchu dialect, for distribution throughout China. He received £200 a year, plus his expenses, and his duties were to find the printers, buy the paper, and direct the setting-up of the type. The work was successfully carried out, but unfortunately when the Bibles were ready for distribution it was discovered that the Manchu dialect was not understood in China, even the Manchus themselves preferring to use Chinese. This small oversight cost the Bible Society £2,600.

Borrow was recalled and sent to spread the Gospel in Spain. He did this with great success, selling a large number of New Testaments in spite of opposition from the Roman Catholic Church. One fears that his success was less due to his missionary zeal than to a plausible tongue and a gipsyish love of wandering; for when he had first left Norwich and come to London he had stoutly affirmed his intention to 'write plays, poetry, etc., abuse religion, and get myself prosecuted.' Perhaps poverty had destroyed this beautiful Shelleyan idealism; perhaps he simply found that it was more fun to sell Bibles.

While he was in Spain, Borrow married a widow, Mary Clarke, whom he had known for some years in England. She followed him to Seville determined to marry him, and Borrow put up little or no resistance. She was possessed of a considerable estate.

When he returned to England, Borrow used his letters to the Bible Society as the basis for a book entitled *The Bible in Spain*. It thoroughly deserved the success it achieved, being spirited and entertaining and crammed from beginning to end with magnificent lies. Encouraged by its reception, Borrow wrote the story of his life, *Lavengro* (published in 1851, eight years after *The Bible in Spain*), and followed it in 1857 with a sequel, *The Romany Rye*. Both books were failures. They did not suit their age; for they told of the open road at a time when England was thinking in terms of railway-lines, of the empty heath when the prosperous new industrialists were only interested in factory sites, of prize-fights and gipsies in a period when respectability was measured by the size of drawing-rooms and the quality of the red-plush seats on the chairs. . . . The Victorians would tolerate *The Bible in Spain* because it had a respectable title, because Mr. Gladstone and Sir Robert Peel approved it, perhaps because the zealousness of missionaries and the wide diffusion of the Bible had had a great deal to do with their present prosperity. But *Lavengro* was a very different proposition. The wind on the heath blew too gustily through it, and the Victorians, who loved their own hearthstones, had little sympathy for the Romany people who dwelt in tents and who did not even seem to desire the comfortable security and stability of a home. Mr. Petulengro, who wanted none of the solid material things which the manufacturers worshipped, who cared nothing for money nor for rich possessions nor for the ownership of land, must have seemed an almost anarchic figure to the good Victorians. He was powerless to harm them, so they did not regard him as dangerous, though his scorn of possessions almost amounted to blasphemy. They smiled and dismissed the thought of him with a nod. . . . *Lavengro* fell as flat as a pancake.

But now the wheel has come full-circle. Most of us, I think, would be disposed to envy Mr. Petulengro and the rest of the Romany people; for the great Victorian bubble has burst, and we have discovered that vast possessions have a way of getting their own back on their owners in the end. To-day we have got almost all the things that the Victorians wanted: swift railways, factories beyond their dreams, enormous towns, rural 'development,' and new machines which they never even thought of; yet there are very few of us who would confidently assert that we are better off than the gipsies. We have lost the cocksure materialism that believed machines indispensable and science infallible; the machines and the scientists have become our masters, and we would be rid of them if we knew how. We don't know how, and so we envy the wandering roofless people who owe no allegiance to such masters, who stand outside our complex modern State, who are unaffected by our politics and whom even our wars do not concern. Overwhelmed by bureaucracy, we wish for nothing better than to be as free as the gipsies; but we might just as well wish for the moon.

Lavengro was written about fifty years too early. I believe that if it had come out in 1901 it would have sold fifty thousand copies. As it was, it took twenty years to sell three thousand. Nobody was interested in the gipsies, and hardly anybody was interested in the story of Mr. Borrow's life, which in any case they would have been disinclined to believe. And with reason; for *Lavengro*, which began as a sober autobiography, blossomed before long into the full flower of fiction, and eventually got so far away from the truth that when its sequel—*The Romany Rye*—appeared, its author was compelled to disclaim any attempt at autobiography at all. However, that doesn't matter to us; for had we been given the truth, the whole truth, and nothing but the truth we should have known nothing, I fear, of the glorious fight between Lavengro and the Flaming Tinman, nor of Mrs. Herne and the poisoned cakes, nor of many other exciting things which in all probability never occurred.

And should we, I wonder, if Borrow had aimed at being as accurate as Hansard, have ever heard that famous scrap of dialogue which might have been whispered by the cool sweet wind that blows off the hill?

'When a man dies, he is cast into the earth,

and his wife and child sorrow over him. If he has neither wife nor child, then his father and mother, I suppose; and if he is quite alone in the world, why, then, he is cast into the earth, and there is an end of the matter.'

'And do you think that is the end of man?'

'There 's an end of him, brother, more 's the pity.'

'Why do you say so?'

'Life is sweet, brother.'

'Do you think so?'

'Think so!—There 's night and day, brother, both sweet things; sun, moon, and stars, brother, all sweet things; there 's likewise a wind on the heath. Life is very sweet, brother; who would wish to die?'

'I would wish to die——'

'You talk like a gorgio—which is the same as talking like a fool—were you a Rommany chal you would talk wiser. Wish to die, indeed!—A Rommany chal would wish to live for ever!'

'In sickness, Jasper?'

'There 's the sun and the stars, brother.'

'In blindness, Jasper?'

'There 's the wind on the heath, brother; if I could only feel that, I would gladly live for ever. Dosta, we 'll now go to the tents and put on the gloves; and I 'll try to make you feel what a good thing it is to be alive, brother!'

No wonder the Victorians did not like *Lavengro*; the Romany philosophy was not for them. They loved riches so much that they could not believe that death was like the snuffing out of a candle, they could not face the prospect of being parted from riches for all eternity. So they laid up a store of riches in heaven, and steadfastly believed that when they died they would inherit them. Mr. Petulengro, who owned hardly anything in this world and who expected nothing in the next—who asked nothing more than the wind and the stars which were free to all men—he was scarcely the right philosopher for them!

In 1862 Borrow published his fourth and last important work, *Wild Wales*. It is less like the account of a man's walking-tour than like the journal of a great blustering gale blowing up hill and down dale from end to end of the Principality. Borrow doesn't walk; he blows along at a pace which can only be indicated by means of the Beaufort Scale. He blusters into inns and curses their bad beer in the name of the great bard Sion Tudor, who was in the habit of making up poems about bad beer; he disputes about religion with people he meets on the road; he tells the Welsh they don't know their own language; he teaches the gipsies how to sing their

National Portrait Gallery

GEORGE BORROW
(J. T. Borrow)

own songs; he goes up Snowdon like a hurricane, and at the summit, which is sacred to the Muses, he thunders out Welsh poetry at the top of his voice, with none but the flying clouds for audience.

It is all tremendously virile, splendidly alive, and sometimes a little irritating. Borrow's voice shouts at one in *Wild Wales* just as Cobbett's John-Bullish roar shouts at one in *Rural Rides*; and although one doesn't mind it on a mountain-top, one finds it a trifle embarrassing within four walls. When the door of a bar-parlour opens, and Borrow comes in like the north wind, one cannot help feeling a little sorry for the unfortunate Welshmen who are now condemned to listen for several hours to a loud discourse on the subject of one of their own bards whom they have probably never heard of; and then, as likely as not, to be cursed roundly at the end of it for neglecting a national masterpiece. But when Borrow is in the open air, and particularly when he has the gipsy people for company, his talk is good talk, and one can listen to it without embarrassment. *Lavengro* is a better book than *Wild Wales*, because it contains several unforgettable characters—Isopel Berners, the Flaming Tinman, Mrs. Herne with her 'brimstoneness of disposition,' Leonora, Mr. Petulengro—whereas the only unforgettable character in *Wild Wales* is George Borrow himself, and he is so obtrusive

M

that one would give anything to be allowed to forget him.

Wild Wales fell even flatter than its predecessors; only a thousand copies were sold. Once again Borrow was unlucky in his age; for it was not until fifty years later that Englishmen discovered the Open Road, and walking became so much the fashion that it was almost obligatory for men of letters to indulge in it. Those glorious days when Edward Thomas tramped along the Icknield Way, when Mr. Belloc bestrode the Sussex Downs like a colossus, when even Mr. G. K. Chesterton panted from pub to pub and sang undying praises of the brown beer—they would have suited Borrow very well. As it was, he was a very lonely pedestrian. Walking was another thing that seemed hardly respectable to the Victorians; perhaps it, too, savoured of anarchy—at the dawn of the Railway Age! There was something a little tactless, at that particular time, in Borrow's virile demonstration that it was possible to get along quite well without the aid of a machine. Man's new altars were the blast furnaces of the north; and it was as if Borrow mocked them when he strode up Snowdon and worshipped the Muses upon its summit.

So *Wild Wales* failed for much the same reasons

as those for which *Lavengro* and *The Romany Rye* failed; and Borrow, bewildered, angry, and bitterly disappointed, wrote little more. He went to live in London and continued his vast and rather futile philological studies, acquiring with the aid of a stupendous memory a working knowledge of almost every language under the sun; and he made a few friends, including Dr. Hake and Theodore Watts-Dunton. But his wife died in 1869, and his last twelve years were darkened by sorrow. He retired from London to Oulton Broad in Norfolk and became a sort of recluse; it is said that towards the end he fell, like his father before him, into a deep religious melancholy. Thus he rather dismally lingered on, old, eccentric, and obscure, until the 26th of July 1881, when he died, suffocated to death by the musty air of Victorian respectability into which he had fallen. The Scholar Gipsy who had always known in his heart of hearts that it was better to be a gipsy than to be a scholar had succumbed in his later days to the blighting influence of his period. The Victorians had won.

Chapter 10 *The Eagle and the Caged Bird*

At the beginning of *Nature in Downland*, W. H. Hudson relates a strange and disturbing encounter which occurred to him in the village of Goring, where Richard Jefferies died. On a cloudy melancholy day in September, Hudson was looking for Jefferies's cottage and thinking much about him 'who had doubtless often walked here too, feeling the icy hand on him of one that walked invisible at his side.' Suddenly he heard the crunching of gravel beneath other feet than his own, and behold 'there before me stood the man himself, back on earth in the guise of a tramp! It was a most extraordinary coincidence that at such a moment I should have come face to face with this poor outcast and wanderer who had the Jefferies countenance as I knew it from portraits and descriptions. It was the long thoughtful suffering face, long straight nose, flowing brown beard, and rather large full blue eyes. I was startled at the expression, the unmistakable stamp of a misery that was anguish and near to despair and insanity. He passed me, then paused, and after a moment or two, said hesitatingly: "Can you spare a penny?" I gave him something without looking at his face again, and went on my way sorry that I had met him, for I knew that those miserable eyes would continue to haunt me.'

This queer meeting that was not a meeting at all was the only occasion when the two naturalists came face to face; for Hudson never saw Jefferies during his life-time. Jefferies had been dead twelve years when Hudson, for a brief moment of time, looked into his haunted melancholy eyes. What he saw there he pitied, and did not much care to think about. One wonders what Jefferies would have seen if he could have looked at Hudson through the eyes of that unexplained, accidental tramp. Nothing to pity and much to envy, I think. . . . Hudson stood six foot three, and stooped a little, as if he feared that his great head would brush the heavens. He had big ears, deep-set penetrating hazel eyes, heavy eyebrows, and a large hawk-like nose; his hair and beard were grizzled like an old badger's pelt; he had long arms and big hands. But those are mere words; and there was about Hudson an air and spirit which no description of form and feature can express. In the street (says Morley Roberts) 'he was as noticeable and as much noted as if he had been an inhabitant of another planet.' His whole appearance was somehow aquiline; he looked as if he might at any moment take to the skies 'and return no more to those earth-bound creatures with whom he had made his temporary home.' Poor sick Jefferies, crushed by the world, would have envied such soaring freedom, such a strong-winged spirit. Perhaps (because he was very gentle) he would have feared it too.

Hudson came to London from the wide grassy pampa that borders the Gran Chaco in the year 1869, when Jefferies was struggling vainly and obscurely for a living and a name. There were many years of struggle in front of Hudson too: years of wretchedness and poverty in a great city which he hated. But circumstances could not hurt him as they hurt poor Jefferies. The caged linnet fears its jailers; the captive eagle, bitter and proud, always regards them as beings very inferior to itself.

Hudson's situation in London was a strange and horrible one for a man who possessed so many of the qualities of such a bird. He had known the huge distances of the Argentine pampas; now, from his window, he could see only a few yards across a dingy street. He had had for company the horses, the wild cattle, the rough free gauchos; now he sat at table with a few dried-up elderly spinsters, with 'ladies in reduced circumstances,' with dim little clerks whose clean collars (pathetically rubbed with bread-crumbs to make them last a week) were the outward and visible sign of the respectability which they sought so painfully to attain. Hudson lived for several years in an impoverished and unsuccessful boarding-house, kept by his wife.

In the East End or the West End he would have been more at home; one can dimly see him in Mayfair, one can more easily picture him in the neighbourhood of the docks, where perhaps he might have made himself into an uncrowned king of the beggars, like Flecker's Rafi. The eagle seems to demand a background either of glory or of high tragedy; one shrinks from the contemplation of this rather shabby eagle, dragging out its existence in the colourless and unspectacular atmosphere of Leinster Square. Yet there Hudson lived, with the old ladies and the clerks and the faded wall-paper, until his wife's boarding-house failed because its dingy clientèle could not pay their bills; and then he moved to another, until that also failed; and so again. Whether it was due to mismanagement or to softness of heart, Emily Hudson's dismal ventures always, inevitably, failed.

It is much easier, and for some strange reason much pleasanter, to picture Genius starving in an attic than to see Genius eking out existence on boiled scraggy mutton and burnt rice pudding in a suburban dining-room. One feels that its diet should be caviare and nightingales' tongues or dry bread and water; nothing less and nothing more. One's sense of the picturesque is cheated by the dingier shades of poverty. Again, having performed the difficult feat of imagining Genius in such a painful and undignified situation, one expects from Genius some spectacular protest, some glorious gesture of passion or escape, the heaven-born anger of an outraged god. At the very least, the rice pudding should be thrown at its donor's head; and when Genius sits down meekly and uncomplainingly and eats the rice pudding, one feels that one has been cheated again. The spectacle is too painful to be watched.

It is disappointingly true that Hudson accepted and endured his squalid surroundings, his dingy company, his poverty, and the repeated failures of his wife's petty venture without making any of the gestures of Genius misused. He neither cried his wrongs to high heaven nor poetically died of consumption. He went on writing, steadily and unsuccessfully, in some of the most lucent English prose that has ever been written, and whenever he could spare a few shillings for a railway fare he went out into the country and watched birds.

Jefferies, in such a situation, would have died of a broken heart or lost his reason; but Hudson was very much tougher than Jefferies, and moreover he was a trained scientist, whereas Jefferies was ever a sentimentalist. The scientific attitude can be a strong armour against the world, for even the unfriendliest of men, the most faithless of lovers, the most persistent of creditors, if regarded in the light of dispassionate scientific inquiry, becomes of no more account than a species of bat or of beetle.

Hudson's approach to human beings was that of a naturalist. When he walked in the country he studied the habits of birds; when he walked in the town he applied the same methods to the study of his fellow-men. His attitude to an owl in a coppice or a passer-by in a street was in each case an attitude of aloof scientific interest. The former was a specimen of *Flammea flammea*, the latter merely another example of *Homo sapiens*. As such, both were worthy of study; and if perchance the relationship was to be continued on a different footing, then the owl, of the two, was the more likely to become Hudson's congenial friend.

That was his attitude to an unfriendly world. He had more affection and more pity for the birds and beasts than he had for his fellow-men. The sight of an owl in captivity (he was particularly fond of owls) would invariably provoke in him a passionate anger; he would move heaven and earth to release it. Yet the spectacle of the broken, ruined men of drink-sodden Chichester, which he describes so savagely in *Nature in Downland*, awakened no pity in him, only loathing and contempt. 'In the streets, near the Railway Station, at the Market Cross, you will see groups of the most utterly drink-degraded wretches it is possible to find anywhere in the kingdom—men with soulless bloated faces and watery eyes, dressed like tramps—standing idle with their hands in their pockets. But there is not a penny there, or they would not be standing in the mud and the rain; and as for doing any work, they are past that. Here that rare spectacle, a man without a shirt, has met my sight, not once nor twice, but several times, the naked flesh showing through the rents of a ragged jacket buttoned or pinned up to the neck. These loathly human objects are strangely incongruous at that spot, under the great spire, in sight of the green open healthy downs, in perhaps the richest agricultural district in England.' No pity there! But compare the sensitive and moving passage about the caged owl, which occurs only a few pages later: 'He was kept in an always malodorous and usually uncovered cage, in the kitchen, where a big fire was burning sixteen to seventeen hours every day. The heat must have been—and alas! still must be—dreadful to the poor bird; but if speech had been given him he would, I think, have complained most of the gas-jets; they were burning all about him until twelve o'clock at night, and the sensation they produced must have been as of fine heated needles, heated red and heated white, stabbing and pricking his sensitive eyeballs. In this chamber of torture the miserable bird had existed for nine months. . . .'

'There is no reason, no excuse to be made, for confining him,' bursts out Hudson angrily. 'He does not sing and twitter, nor amuse his jailer with lively motions and brilliant colour. Beautiful to see when flying at sunset about the village and farm where he is not persecuted, and grotesque beyond description when viewed by day in his dimly-lighted loft or tower, rocking his body to and fro, now crouching cat-like, then stretching himself up, and all the time making strange weird faces at you, in a cage he is a most pitiful spectacle, a depressed, dead-alive-looking white owl, no longer white, his beautiful plumage smirched and disarranged.

> A robin redbreast in a cage
> Puts all heaven in a rage,

said Blake; and a white owl in a cage must produce the same effect, if we may indeed believe that unearthly eyes regard us, and see the fantastic tricks which we play with our unhappy fellow-creatures.'

Hudson did everything he could to secure the bird's release. He pleaded, he cajoled, he even offered out of his poverty whatever sum its owner might ask in return for its freedom. He failed; and he recorded his failure in a passage which is alight with a terrible anger and a terrible pity, a passage in which, like a prophet of old, he prayed vengeance from the pitiless gods against the unwitting ill-doer.

'She would not part with the bird for love or money. Up till then I had visited the bird every day, and opening its cage would put my hand in to caress it. It liked to be gently stroked on the breast, and when caressed in this way would play with my fingers, biting them but very gently with its beak. But from that time I was ashamed to go near him, or even to look at him; for I had promised him his liberty, and could not keep my word. Nor was it necessary that I should look at to see him; his melancholy image was too deeply graved in my mind—a feathered Dreyfus, Semitic features and all, the head bowed, the weary eyes closed, the hooked nose just visible amidst a wilderness of white whiskers. I could only try to believe that there is some foundation for the ancient belief held in so many lands, that the owl is indeed a supernatural, or sacred, bird; that when this captive had been tortured to death and its carcass thrown into the dust-heap, the loving-kindness that had been shown to him would have swift and suitable reward.'

Already the drunken men of Chichester were forgotten, ousted from Hudson's mind by the torturing memory of that grave dignified bird, so quiet and yet so restless in his cage. Mankind could look after itself; its revolting condition was the direct result of its own grotesque follies. Those street-corner Calibans got no pity from Hudson. They were ugly and they were incomprehensible and they were fools; and the birds were never that, until men's cruelties made them so.

Hudson, who was wiser than any man in the ways of the wild creatures, found nothing strange in Nature, but much that was strange in mankind. Nature's cruelties he could understand—had he not watched the *caranchos,* the high-soaring, ever-watchful vultures, following the sick and laggard beast on the Argentine plains ?—but man's cruelties he found incomprehensible and disgusting. He saw in Nature a plan, an order, that might or might not be divine; in mankind the order dissolved into chaos, the plan was distorted and parodied, and as for divinity, if God had made the snakes and the owls and the badgers and the foxes, then the devil had had the marring of man. Hudson did not believe in the Immortal Soul.

He was curiously ungentle in his dealings with his fellow-men—he who was so gentle with the birds and the beasts. He was often rough, intolerant, sometimes downright rude; he hated fools, hypocrites, puritans, prudes, mountebanks, and human brutes, and having, as it were, examined one of these and found that it belonged to a common and unpleasing subspecies of *Homo sapiens,* he took no more interest in it than he would have done in a sparrow which he had mistaken for something rarer. His relations with women (even in the most intimate sense) were tinged with the same strange aloofness. He needed women now and then, and he agreed with the Spanish saying which he must have heard from the gauchos in his youth, *Pecado de carne no es pecado*; but he never, as far as we know, fell in love with them, and he probably regarded them also as specimens—the female of the species, and therefore useful for the fulfilment of the principal purpose for which the female was designed. Who they were, and what they thought about it, we do not know; but it is not unreasonable to hazard that the bats and the birds which he handled, the snakes which he picked up on the Downs, knew more about Hudson than they did. His gentleness was always reserved for the wild, timid things.

And, to them, who has ever been gentler? There is a paragraph in *The Book of a Naturalist* in which Hudson describes a bat's wing as the most sensitive thing in Nature, barring the antennae of insects. It is 'a bed and field of nerves, so closely placed as to give the membrane the appearance of the finest, softest shot silk. The brains of the creature, as it were, are carried spread out on its wings, and so exquisitively delicate is the sensitiveness of these parts that in comparison our finger-tips are no more quick of feeling than the thick tough hide of some lumbering pachyderm. I have handled scores of bats in my time, and have never had one in my hand without being struck by its shrinking, shivering motions, the tremors that passed over it like wave following wave, and it has seemed to me that the touch of a soft finger-tip on its wing was to the bat like the blow of a cheese- or bread-grater on his naked body to a man.'

He took pains to learn how to hold his specimens so that he hurt them as little as possible, or not at all. He even taught himself how to pick up the vicious, whippy, quick-striking adders, gripping them firmly by the back of the head so that a sort of armed neutrality was observed between the snake and its captor, the hissing, flickering tongue of the former threatening deadly poison in vain and the firm yet gentle hand of the latter quietly persuading: 'Be still while I measure you, and I'll let you go in peace.' Hudson loved these 'wild wormes in woods,' and he often hunted them on the Downs and in the New Forest, searching eagerly for the rare sort which has a turquoise or forget-me-not blue belly of a particularly beautiful shade. Describing one of these, he wrote in a chapter called 'Hints to Adder-seekers': 'It reminded me rather of the most exquisite blue one has seen on some priceless piece of old Chinese pottery. I think that if some famous aged artist of the great period, a worshipper of colour whose life had been spent in the long endeavour to capture and make permanent the most exquisite fleeting tints in Nature, had seen the blue on that adder he would have been overcome at the same time with rapture and despair.'

National Portrait Gallery

W. H. HUDSON

(Sir W. Rothenstein)

He let the little creature go, declaring that the finding of it had been 'one of the loveliest experiences' he had ever had. Nothing would ever induce him to kill a snake, although he was once compelled to stun, temporarily, an exceptionally large specimen in order that he might measure it. He was not interested, he said, in 'the little rope of clay or dead flesh in the British Museum, coiled in its bottle of spirits, and labelled "*Vipera berus,* Linn."'; what he sought was the live adder, the sun-lover, the silent-moving, swift-striking half-yard of rippling, gaily-painted whipcord, 'and he dwells not in a jar of alcohol in the still shade and equable temperature of a museum.' Ophiologists and herpetologists were anathema to Hudson; for he was that very rare thing, a trained scientist who had not let Science become his master.

When he wrote about birds and beasts he combined the strictest accuracy with the swiftest-winged fancy. He would tell, in a chapter about hawk-moths, of '*Acherontia atropos* going about his flowery business,' giving a strange new flavour to his prose by the use of scientific nomenclature in conjunction with such a lovely phrase. But he was no stickler for Latin names, and more than any other writer, before or since, he was able to describe the 'personality,' as it were, of some wild thing by means of the one perfect English adjective. (I think that no modern writer, except perhaps D. H. Lawrence, has ever used adjectives as beautifully as Hudson did.) Thus he writes of 'gipsy foxes'—and could the handsome, slinking, stealing red fellow be better named?—of 'the strenuous mole' and 'the diabolical weasel' and 'the hermit badger.' The badger, by the way, was one of his favourite animals; strange and fearsome and sublime, it stood out among the little beasts of England. There is a marvellous description in *The Book of a Naturalist* of a midnight meeting between a badger and a rural policeman in west Cornwall, 'a giant six feet six in height, a mighty wrestler, withal a sober, religious man, himself a terror to all evil-doers in the place.' The policeman's beat extended on one side to the border of a wide, wild moor, 'and one very dark night last winter he was at this desolate spot when he heard the distant sound of a horse cantering over the ground. The heavy rains had flooded the land, and he heard the splash of the hoofs as the horse came towards him. "Who could this be out on horseback at twelve o'clock on a dark winter night?" he asked himself; and listened and waited while the sound grew louder and louder and came nearer and nearer, and he strained his eyes to see the figure of a man on horseback emerging from the gloom, and could see nothing. Then it suddenly came into his mind that it was no material horseman, but a spirit accustomed to ride at that hour in that place, and his hair stood up on his head like the bristles on a pig's back. "It almost lifted my helmet off," he confessed, and he would have fled, but his trembling legs refused to move. Then, all at once, when he was about to drop, fainting with extreme terror, the cause of the sound appeared—an old dog badger trotting over the flooded moor, vigorously pounding the water with his feet, and making as much noise as a trotting horse with his hoofs. The badger was seven or eight yards away when he first caught sight of him, and the badger, too, then saw a sublime and terrible creature standing motionless before him, and for a few moments they stared at one another; then the badger turned aside and vanished into the darkness.'

That is a tremendously dramatic moment when the policeman and the badger stand staring at one another, and each sees in the other a sublime and terrible creature that has come out of the dark. All encounters, all contacts, between men and animals seemed to Hudson to contain that element of terror and strangeness. They spoke no common language, they shared no common wisdom or experience, they were beings as incomprehensible to each other as a dweller on this planet would be to a Martian. Hudson had the rare faculty of being able, to a small degree, to look at men through the eyes of the wild animals; and he saw them as they saw them, grotesque, terrifying, fearful, and strange: *ingens et horribile, mirabile dictu.*

When he looked at them through his own eyes they were no longer terrifying, but they were still incomprehensible and strange; they were specimens, but they were specimens which obstinately refused to be classified and catalogued; and their actions were far stranger, far less easy to understand, than the way of a bird in the air.

During his dark years in London, Hudson would walk in the streets and peer at the faces of the passers-by, wondering at them, seeing in their hurried, purposeless movements a comi-tragedy which he could not comprehend. But because they seemed so strange to him, they could not touch him, they could not hurt him, they could not trouble him at all. He remained aloof, aquiline. The paltry reward he received from his writings, the ingratitude of a world that refused to acknowledge him, the injustice of a system that fed mediocrity on caviare and left genius to starve—these things bothered him not at all. (Later, when his books earned him large sums, he had so little use for the money that he gave it away, not to a hospital, not to the poor, but to the Bird Society. Let mankind look after itself!) Self-pity was an indulgence which he hated; it made him feel rather sick, just as poor Jefferies's *Story of my Heart*, with its fear and knowledge of death and its dreadful revelation of a sick soul, made him feel queasy and uncomfortable.

While Hudson was writing his early books in London, Jefferies's lesser lamp was burning itself out; and Jefferies was bitter and disappointed and afraid, because he was a dying man and because the world had been unkind to him. Hudson, who could be gloriously angry at times (chiefly about caged owls, feathers in ladies' hats, and the extinction of rare species), was never bitter, and he never experienced any of the soul-torturing disappointment which Jefferies felt. He had a breadth and depth of vision which Jefferies did not possess. He saw the world and all that in it was from a great height, as if he were indeed a sky-soaring eagle; poor Jefferies, studying his meadow-grasses, saw only a little of it—out of proportion. Jefferies made a small patch of Wiltshire live, in rather laboured, not-very-distinguished prose; he wrote, probably better than any one else, of the humbler country sports, ferreting, rabbit-shooting, and poaching, and of the gamekeeper's round, the dark damp nights in the woods and the dusky autumn evenings when the pheasants clatter up into the trees; and he achieved in *Bevis* (surely his best book) an altogether charming and delightful study of a country boyhood. However, that was the limit of his achievement; he wrote very pleasantly of the country scene, but he was not an original observer, like White and Hudson, and he was spoiled for a scientist by his sentimentality. When the winds of the world blew coldly about him, he degenerated into a sort of unhappy mystic, and later into a full-blown second-rate philosopher, writing a lot of wishy-washy blather about his soul. The tragic writings of Jefferies are almost entirely concerned with himself; whereas Hudson, looking down from his eagle height, saw the whole of Nature, the inter-relation of genera and families, the slow, inevitable crawl of the evolutionary process, culminating in the tragedy of Man. One of the greatest benefits conferred by a scientific education is the consequent realization of one's own comparative unimportance; Hudson could find no tragedy in his own affairs, but he could write majestically of the tragic passing of a whole beautiful species:

'And, above all others, we should protect and hold sacred those types, Nature's masterpieces, which are first singled out for destruction on account of their size, or splendour, or rarity, and that false, detestable glory which is accorded to their most successful slayers. In ancient times the spirit of life shone brightest in these; and, when others that shared the earth with them were taken by death, they were left, being more worthy of perpetuation. Like immortal flowers they have drifted down to us on the ocean of time, and their strangeness and beauty bring to our imaginations a dream and a picture of that unknown world, immeasurably far removed, where man was not: and when they perish, something of gladness goes out from Nature, and the sunshine loses something of its brightness.'

Man was but another species to Hudson; and if this strange mammalian should go the way of the trilobite and the dinosaur in the fullness of evolutionary time—well, he could contemplate the prospect of its passing with no more regret than he felt for the passing of the great auk. After all, it could not match for beauty the rippling swiftness of a snake, the poise of a young gazelle, the delicacy of a humming-bird, the splendour of a lion; and if it had wisdom which none other possessed, if it could tame the fire and the winds and the waters to its purposes, if it could number the stars in the heavens and comprehend the infinite distances of interstellar space, if it could write the tragedies of *Hamlet* and *Macbeth* and *Lear* —what was the use, since that wisdom was employed also to destroy Nature's loveliest and rarest creatures, and to invent the pole-trap, and to cage a white owl till it pined away and died?

Chapter 11 — *The Halcyon Days*

For seven days before the winter solstice (says Pliny), and for as many days after, lasted the *Halcyonides dies*, when the winds ceased to blow and the turbulent seas became still, and the kingfisher launched its nest upon the glassy surface of the ocean. For a fortnight the elements were at peace, while that bright bird sailed about on her buoyant nest and hatched out the eggs she had laid in it; and on the fourteenth day the nest was abandoned, she flew away with her young ones, and the great winds began to roar again, raising once more the fury of the sea.

In England, during the years between 1910 and 1914, it was as if a kingfisher sailed always upon the sea. The world was at peace; and yet at the back of men's minds there lurked, half-felt, half-known, and unspoken, a consciousness of the impending storm. It was as if they sensed the far-away thunder in the cloudless sky, as countrymen will do when they gather their harvest against time in a hot September. England lay outwardly at peace, but with every nerve a-quiver.

It was an atmosphere in which young poets flourished. The Muse had nearly fainted for lack of fresh air in the stuffiness of Victorian drawing-rooms; she had grown sick and acquired a deathly pallor in those later days when the Green Carnation was her strange emblem. But now she became eager and alive in a world in which a young man could smell the distant danger as a war-horse smells far-off blood. While the storm crept up over Europe the poets wrote as if they would indeed make hay while the sun shone—as if they had a foreknowledge that the time for writing was short and would soon be over.

Perhaps it was no coincidence that they wrote, for the most part, of the woods and the meadows and the roads that went between them; for, like timber-trees notched with the axe, many of these young poets were marked to die, and it was of green fields, remember, that Falstaff babbled when his hour came upon him. The profound, the epic, the cosmic things have a queer way of melting into nothing at the imminence of death; they that have seemed so sure and solid flee appalled in that tremendous moment before the one irrefutable Fact besides which nothing is sure; and in their place comes creeping back the memory of trivial, loved things, such as a hayfield of childhood, or a country lane, or a house or a plot of land from which it hurts to be parted. And strangely, when the great certainties have vanished like cowardly battalions which melt before the foe, these very frail weapons can sometimes arm a man against mortality:

> If I should die, think only this of me:
> That there's some corner of a foreign field
> That is for ever England.

Perhaps Rubert Brooke, more clearly than any other of the young poets, heard the far-off thunder of the coming storm. Was it this knowledge that lent such a passionate intensity to his list of the 'little things' in *The Great Lover*, and imparted such an eagerness, such an anxious questioning, to the beautiful last lines of *Grantchester*:

> Is dawn a secret shy and cold
> Anadyomene, silver-gold?
> And sunset still a golden sea
> From Haslingfield to Madingley?
> And after, ere the night is born,
> Do hares come out among the corn?
> Oh, is the water sweet and cool,
> Gentle and brown, above the pool?
> And laughs the immortal river still—
> Under the mill, under the mill?
> Say, is there Beauty yet to find?
> And Certainty? and Quiet kind?

Deep-meadows yet, for to forget
The lies, and truths, and pain . . . oh! yet
Stands the Church clock at ten to three?
And is there honey still for tea?

One feels that all through the poem he is asking for an assurance that these loved things were really certain and secure. 'Or shall I wake up one morning and find that they are nothing, that they have gone?' His doubts were to be realized; for the storm was creeping up, and when it broke there would be no honey for tea.

Meanwhile, however, the young poets gathered in their harvest with an eye to the clouding sky. It was largely a harvest of little things; indeed, it might be said of the Georgians that they would passionately sing the praises of a dandelion or a teacup while the great issues went hang. I think it would be unfair to say it; there are worse gods to worship than *lares* and *penates*, and if divinity is manifest anywhere it is manifest in the springing of a blade of grass; but it is certainly true that the young poets said to themselves, *Forsan et haec olim meminisse juvabit*, and set themselves about storing up a horde of bright memories of small and familiar things against the time when such things would seem very precious and rare, amid the blood and the bullets.

The Elizabethans, stepping forth into an immensely wide world lit by the wondrous sunshine of their age, had gone adventuring into distant realms, finding strange and fantastical islands set in faerie seas; or they had sailed boldly into the sphere of the intellect, and come back with such strange prizes as Donne's *Ecstacy* or Browne's *Religio Medici*. The Augustans had concerned themselves with personalities and the swift sword-play of wits. Shelley had soared into aery regions where even his own skylark became a sort of disembodied spirit, singing nebulous nothings to the sky. Byron had written of the love of woman; Wordsworth had seen in Nature the all-pervading benevolence of the spirit which moved the world; Coleridge had flown to Xanadu on the wings of an opium dream; the great Victorians had chosen themes best suited to their own vast materialism, and the Pre-Raphaelites, in reaction, had written wistfully about their souls. But it was left to the young Georgians who were soon to die to find poetry in the most trivial things about them:

> Firm sands; the little dulling edge of foam
> That browns and dwindles as the wave goes home;
> And washen stones, gay for an hour; the cold
> Graveness of iron; moist black earthen mould;
> Sleep; and high places; footprints in the dew. . . .

Rupert Brooke's *Great Lover* appeared first in the third issue of a quarterly magazine called *New*

Numbers, which was the joint venture of four of the young poets, Mr. Lascelles Abercrombie, Mr. Wilfrid Wilson Gibson, Mr. John Drinkwater, and Brooke himself. It was printed in Gloucester at the offices of the local weekly, and sent out from Dymock, in the neighbourhood of which Mr. Abercrombie and Mr. Gibson had made their homes. Here in the daffodil lands, close to the Redmarley Hills, they were joined by an American poet, Robert Frost, who had already published his first volume, *A Boy's Will*, and was now writing those lovely country poems which were shortly to appear in *North of Boston*—poems which, while they are essentially American, yet somehow seem to match our own West Country very well. (*After Apple-picking*, for instance, has something of the air of a Dymock as well as of a Massachusetts orchard, and *Mending Wall* might tell of English neighbours:

> And on a day we met to walk the line
> And set the wall between us once again.
> We keep the wall between us as we go.
> To each the boulders that have fallen to each.
> And some are loaves and some so nearly balls
> We have to use a spell to make them balance:
> 'Stay where you are until our backs are turned!')

Frost's second book was published in England in 1914, while *New Numbers* was bravely appearing every three months. Probably there was more good poetry written in that momentous year than in any other of the present century.[1] The kingfisher (but how precariously!) still sailed upon the sea. . . .

In 1914, too, the Dymock poets were joined by another, Edward Thomas, who was known at that time chiefly as an essayist and a biographer. Like Mr. Belloc (who was making splendid songs about his Sussex Downs, and writing of his pilgrimages in what is probably the best English prose of a generation), Edward Thomas had walked the roads of England and told the tale of them. He was a countryman, an observer of birds and flowers, a lover of good inns and good beer, a disciple of Hudson and Jefferies (whose biography he had written). But it was not until the late days of 1914, when the war had scattered the young Georgians and ended the brief and glorious life of their venture, *New Numbers*, that he showed himself as a poet too.

Into less than three years he crowded the writing of all his poetry. Like Frost's and most of Brooke's, it was poetry of the little things of the countryside, of the faggots in a heap by the hedge,

[1] The publication of Mr. Cecil Day Lewis's splendid and important poem, *A Time to Dance*, makes it necessary for me to contradict this statement within six weeks of writing it.

of the mistle-thrush singing in a gale, of the herbs with sweet names, like lad's love and traveller's joy and Bridget-in-her-bravery, of digging in the ground, of

small brown birds
Wisely reiterating endlessly
What no man learnt yet, in or out of school.

He could see loveliness in a swede-pile when the gable of clay was taken away from it:

It is a sight more tender-gorgeous
At the wood corner where Winter moans and drips
Than when, in the Valley of the Tombs of Kings,
A boy crawls down into a Pharaoh's tomb
And, first of Christian men, beholds the mummy,
God and monkey, chariot and throne and vase,
Blue pottery, alabaster, and gold.

But dreamless long-dead Amen-hotep lies.
This is a dream of Winter, sweet as Spring.

He loved words as the Elizabethans loved them, as things rare and gorgeous and beautiful in themselves, things

Light as dreams,
Tough as oak,
Precious as gold,
As poppies and corn,
Or an old cloak:
Sweet as our birds
To the ear,

As the burnet rose
In the heat
Of Midsummer:
Strange as the races
Of dead and unborn:
Strange and sweet
Equally,
And familiar,
To the eye,
As the dearest faces
That a man knows,
And as lost homes are.

And because he loved words so, he delighted in the old country names of flowers and fields and places, lovingly playing with them, mixing them with his poetry, making them sing new songs. *Lob,* one of his longest and best poems, is full of them; and of all the poems that have been written in this century, if I could have only one of them for the rest of my life, I think I should choose *Lob,* not because it is the greatest, but because I love it the most.

Edward Thomas took such delight in these old names that he wrote one merry verse that was all about six of them. It is the jolliest, queerest, sweetest thing, and I cannot refrain from quoting it:

If ever I should by chance grow rich
I 'll buy Codham, Cockridden, and Childerditch,
Roses, Pyrgo, and Lapwater,
And let them all to my elder daughter.

The rent I shall ask of her will be only
Each year's first violets, white and lonely,
The first primroses and orchises—
She must find them before I do, that is.
But if she finds a blossom on furze
Without rent that shall all for ever be hers,
Codham, Cockridden, and Childerditch,
Roses, Pyrgo, and Lapwater—
I 'll give them all to my elder daughter.

He wrote, too, better perhaps than any other poet of our time, of the country people who had given the fields their names, of the old wandering man who had

been in England as long as dove and daw,
Calling the wild cherry tree the merry tree,
The rose campion Bridget-in-her-bravery—

of Bob Hayward, who had died long ago and had given his name to Bob's Lane:

Women he liked, did shovel-bearded Bob,
Old Farmer Hayward of the Heath, but he
Loved horses. He himself was like a cob,
And leather-coloured. Also he loved a tree—

and of the Wiltshire private killed in the first year of the War:

This ploughman dead in battle slept out of doors
Many a frozen night, and merrily
Answered staid drinkers, good bedmen, and all bores:
'At Mrs. Greenland's Hawthorn Bush,' said he,

'I slept.' None knew which bush. Above the town,
Beyond 'The Drover,' a hundred spot the down
In Wiltshire. And where now at last he sleeps
More sound in France—that, too, he secret keeps.

In June of 1915 Thomas himself joined the army. By then the young poets were already scattered. Frost had gone back to America, Gibson was soldiering, Rupert Brooke, the Kit Marlowe of their company, was dead at Lemnos. The daffodils still danced beside the Leadon when the March winds blew, the meadowsweet in June still shed its melancholy perfume upon the quiet air, the dog-roses in the hedgerow, which Thomas had seen 'like mouths' in the dusky bat-light, still bloomed in the deep red lanes of that friendly countryside; but the Dymock poets who had loved these things were gone for ever, and no summer evening spell of hayfields and honeysuckle could call them back again.

Edward Thomas, who had joined up as a private in the Artists' Rifles, soon went to France as a lieutenant of the Royal Artillery, and he was killed at the Battle of Arras on Easter Monday 1917. He was probably the best poet of his generation; if he had lived he might have been one of the best poets of an age. But the storm had swallowed him up, and the brief song of the Georgians was over. Perhaps there had been nothing very profound about it; but it had been a good song all the same, in praise of the English soil and the sweet things which spring from it, and the blessedness of country quietude, in the days when the kingfisher sailed upon the sea.

Chapter 12 *Conclusion*

It was the sudden accident of war that ended the song of the Georgians; slower changes, working gradually but no less inevitably, have altered almost beyond recognition the countryside which they rediscovered with such an eagerness and such a poetic surprise. I don't know where those fields may be which Edward Thomas wanted to let to his elder daughter; but it is at least possible that they are built over now, and that only the oldest of the old men remember them by their old sweet names any longer. Roses, Pyrgo, and Lapwater are titles which would be unlikely to survive in a modern building estate; and who knows what Hill Views, what Lilac Groves, what red-roofed Laburnum Villas may have supplanted them?

And if Codham, Cockridden, and Childerditch

have by chance escaped the jerry-builder, how shall we say that they are still the fine fat pastures that Edward Thomas knew? Are they still worth so princely a rental as the spring's first flowers? Or are they brambly wastes uncared for, with the hedges unlaid and the gateways flooded and the drains broken so that a hundred feggy tufts have sprung up in a dozen marshy places?

Alas, it may be so; for since the halcyon days were over, the winds have blown hard and coldly over the green fields of England. The War, that scattered the young poets, marked the end of a chapter; it may be that it also marked the end of the thing we used to mean by English country life. Various economic causes have combined to rob that particular form of existence of the dignity and quietude which once belonged to it. To-day it is at best a wretched scramble to make ends meet and at worst it is bankruptcy and disaster. One can no longer quote '*O fortunatos nimium!* . . .'; for the silly swain lives, not securer, but more precariously, than his fellows in the towns. He struggles for existence in a tumbledown, haunted No Man's Land where often the crops are not worth harvesting and the stock not worth selling, and where the wind moans sadly through the holes in the roofs of the byres which he cannot afford to repair.

Yes, the chapter ended when the wide stubbles ceased to be, when the wheat-lands and the partridge-lands which Mr. Street so admirably recalls in his splendid *Farmer's Glory* grew less and less, as if the economic forces were whittling them away; and it is fitting that my book about Country Men should end there too. True enough, she still has her chroniclers, this poor broken land. Mr. W. H. Davies, one of the last of the Georgians, still sings of the simple country things with something of the freshness of a thrush at dawning; and Mr. Blunden tells again the same slow, quiet, bitter-sweet tale that John Clare told long ago. A few novelists, too, have made little corners of the land their own and go on writing about them lovingly and well. Mr. John Buchan has the Scottish Highlands, Mr. Francis Brett Young the Severn Valley and the cherry orchards of north Worcestershire, and Mr. Henry Williamson the country of the three rivers. Then Mr. H. J. Massingham, in *Wold Without End,* has done for the district round Chipping Camden the same sort of thing that White did for Selborne; and Mr. Adrian Bell, in the trilogy consisting of *Corduroy, The Cherry Tree,* and *Silver Ley,* has achieved a lovely pastoral in the most delicate and delicious prose—a sort of *Georgics* of the present day.

Yet most of these writers chronicle something which is passing or has already past. They are the historians and the geographers of a changing scene. Mr. Buchan's deer forests may soon be planted with conifers; Birmingham is stretching out its tentacles towards Mr. Brett Young's Clent Hills; Chipping Camden is likely to become little better than a bait for American tourists; even Mr. Williamson's otters may not survive many more generations of polluted rivers; and as for Mr. Bell's farm, its tragedy has been recorded by Mr. Hilaire Belloc (writing of another country-side) in his sad and beautiful lines on *Hannaker Mill*:

> Hannaker Hill is in desolation;
>   Ruin a-top and a field unploughed.
> And Spirits that call on a falling nation,
>   Spirits that loved her calling aloud,
>   Spirits abroad in a windy cloud.
>
> Spirits that call and no one answers—
>   Hannaker 's down and England 's done.
> Wind and thistle for pipe and dancers,
>   And never a ploughman under the sun,
>   Never a ploughman, never a one.

It seems that the men who babble of England's green fields to-day can do little but record the manner of their passing and recollect in tranquillity the beauty and the richness of their past;

but there is nothing very epic about the sort of slow disaster which is creeping gradually over the countryside, and it may be that soon men will cease to listen to the tale of it. In a world that has gone whoring after new things, a chronicler of the happenings of wood and hill and hedgerow has no place; for nothing new happens when the leaves fall in the autumn and when the first flowers come out in the spring. The poets of our time have found other things to concern them: the vast realms of physics where new and strange discoveries are made every day, the regions of the air, and beyond it the whirling planets and the unnumbered stars. Theirs to explore are the terrifying, unmapped territories of the mind; theirs to sing are the great machines. Will there not come a time, I wonder, when in the mighty roar of those machines we forget to listen to the blackbird, and when, as we sail through the skies on wings of incredible swiftness and the green fields seem no more than a patchwork below us, we forget that there are blades of grass springing in those fields, and the first buttercups, and the cuckoo-flowers?

TEWKESBURY,
1933–5

INDEX